Children Can't Wait: Reducing Delays for Children in Foster Care

edited by
Katharine Cahn and Paul Johnson

Child Welfare League of America, Inc.
440 First Street, NW, Suite 310, Washington, DC 20001-2085

Current Printing (last digit)
10 9 8 7 6 5 4 3 2 1

Cover design by S. Dmitri Lipczenko
Text design and composition by AlphaTechnologies/MPS

Printed in the United States of America

ISBN # 0-87868-510-3

Contents

Acknowledgments

The vision for this volume grew from conversations with the contributors and with Jake Terpstra and Carolyn Thompson of the Children's Bureau, U.S. Department of Health and Human Services. We are grateful for their support, ideas, and advice as we share this vision with you.

We are also thankful for the support and patience of the editing and publishing staff of the Child Welfare League of America.

As the authors shared their respective improvements in permanency planning in each of their states, we found many similarities in our improvements and a common commitment to speeding permanency planning for children and families. We wish to applaud the work of the public child welfare professionals, the attorneys, and the community professionals and volunteers who endeavor to provide the best practice available for each child in need of a permanent home.

Paul Johnson
Katharine Cahn

CHAPTER 1

Critical Issues in Permanency Planning: An Overview

Katharine Cahn and Paul Johnson

A safe, permanent home for every child is the mandated goal of child welfare policy. Despite passage of Public Law 96–272, the Adoption Assistance and Child Welfare Act of 1980, the service delivery system continues to fall far short of this goal. In many areas of the country, long-term foster placement or guardianship has become the path of least resistance—a de facto permanent plan. Children are still spending too much time away from persons they consider family.

Although national data are highly unreliable, and variations occur from state to state, it is estimated that the average child entering out-of-home care will remain for three years. Baseline data collected through the projects reviewed in this book support that estimate. Child development specialists agree that the ability to form lasting bonds with any caregiver is severely reduced if a child undergoes too many separations or lingers in impermanence too long. By allowing impermanence for abused or neglected children in our care we are causing further damage. We are damaging children's capacity to form the lasting ties that make families secure and safe.

The mandate of a safe, permanent home for every child is not addressed to the child welfare agency alone. While public child welfare agencies and their subcontracted child-placement agencies carry out case management activities, others are also involved. Courts, judges, lawyers, therapists, foster parents, and a network

1

of citizen advocates and reviewers all contribute to case planning for children. Ironically, the very fact that there are so many concerned parties may increase delays for children.

This book is about reducing delays for children in foster care. It is based on the work of four federally funded projects that successfully reduced delays for children headed for adoption. Although the four projects took four different approaches to the challenge, all of their findings have wide application. Children do not need to wait three years for a permanent home in any of our states.

The System: An Overview

The decision to terminate parental rights is a very serious one, and is treated seriously in juvenile law and child welfare policy. A quick overview of the steps that bring a case to this drastic measure follows.

The child welfare system operates with the intent to keep children safe in their own original families whenever possible. Most states have accepted federal foster care reimbursement and so operate under the requirements of P.L. 96–272, which mandates reasonable efforts to preserve or to quickly reunify the biological families of children in family foster care.

Recognizing the urgency of a child's developmental timeline, the act states that every child must have a permanent plan (adoption or return home) after 18 months in care. It is the federal intent that parents be given time and support to improve, but not unlimited time. Young lives may be put on hold, but not forever.

Because decision-making for families is complex, it involves many service delivery systems. Children in abusive or neglectful situations come to the attention of a child welfare agency through referrals from teachers, medical professionals, police, or concerned neighbors and relatives. The initial job of intervening and strengthening families or removing children from unsafe homes is given to child welfare agencies. If initial efforts to resolve the crisis are not effective, a child can be declared dependent and placed away from home.

The decision for an out-of-home placement is serious enough to trigger a system of checks and balances. While brought by a petition from a social worker and eventually carried to court by an attorney representing the social worker or the public interest, the declaration is subject to challenge from parents and must be approved by a judge. In some jurisdictions an independent advocate, usually called a court-appointed special advocate (CASA) or a guardian ad litem (GAL), may be assigned to represent the rights of the child.

Once a child is in placement with a child welfare agency, services are offered to reunify the family. These may include a continuation of the services that were offered to prevent placement, as well as new efforts to mitigate the need for placement. According to P.L. 96–272, the case plan must be reviewed every six months, with a permanent plan established by the eighteenth month. This review process calls upon judges, lawyers (for the child and for the parent), social welfare agencies working with the parents, and CASAs, GALs, or citizen reviewers. The overlaps among these professional systems provide safeguards for families, a range of expertise, and a sense of urgency to determine the plan.

Again, however, overlapping systems can also be a source of delay, frustration, and confusion in case planning. Child welfare caseworkers complain that they spend more time in review hearings and completing paperwork than they do in face-to-face contact with children and families. Conferences, hearings, and appeals can delay decision-making and prolong foster care stays for children.

The overlap of systems continues for the life of the case. If the conditions that led to removal and placement of the child have not improved, after reasonable efforts have been made to reunite children and parents, the law provides for the termination of parental rights (or TPR), legally freeing the child for adoption. The seriousness of this permanency planning decision again calls all the actors onto the stage: social workers, expert witnesses, advocates, lawyers for all sides, and the judge. The process is designed to be adversarial and to air conflicting opinions.

The final decision can be appealed. In some states, such as New York, appeals are routinely filed on TPR orders. Depending on the number of courts of appeal available, this process can keep a child in limbo for another two to five years.

In 1989 and 1990, the Children's Bureau of the Administration for Children, Youth, and Families within the United States Department of Health and Human Services used Adoption Opportunities funds (discretionary grants awarded periodically by the federal Department of Social and Health Services) to support four projects. These four projects produced results for children in care whose permanent plan was adoption by improving case planning and reducing delays. This book describes for other professionals the critical issues these projects identified and some of their useful strategies.

The Projects: An Overview

The Adoption Opportunities grants were intended to reduce the length of time children waited to be legally free by resolving problems between courts and agencies—that is, between attorneys and social workers. Each project succeeded in producing more timely permanence for children in care.

In Michigan, grant funds supported legal assistance for caseworkers from the very start of cases with TPR potential, allowing better case preparation for both the social worker and the attorney. Cases were successfully resolved much earlier than the national average, so that children in Michigan can now expect permanent homes relatively quickly. Children in Michigan have also benefited from the shorter timelines for decision-making established by state statute. The chapter on the Michigan experience demonstrates how changing the laws can help children.

In two New York counties, a lawyer from the American Bar Association worked with social workers to review cases and determine which changes in practice would most effectively reduce delays. New procedures and a new approach to training altered agency practice. The chapter on this experience emphasizes case preparation approaches that social workers can carry out in a public child welfare agency setting.

In Kentucky, the governor sponsored a task force of top administrators from key agencies to develop interagency solutions. This chapter illustrates the value of interagency collaboration from the top down, and offers a model for strategic planning to bring it about. Most notable are the use of training and the development of a common information management system to improve practice.

In the Pacific Northwest, the project produced local seminars where professionals could work together to identify the problems causing delays in their counties and then to solve them. The locally generated systems improvements this interagency action planning fostered were responsible for clearing up backlogged cases in nine counties.

Each project included a phase when the source of delays was located. In state after state, the same critical issues were found to be impeding timely permanency planning. These findings, while hardly surprising to those who work in this field, constitute important starting points for anyone intent on improving the lot of children in care.

Critical Issues

Confusion about "Reasonable Efforts"

Across the country, there is a lack of legal and professional consensus on what *reasonable* means, in the phrase *reasonable efforts,* and whether reasonable efforts should be the standard for granting TPR petitions. Public Law 96–272 requires the child welfare agency to make reasonable efforts to preserve or to reunify the family of every child in foster care receiving federal funds. Many states have written this reasonable efforts standard into their TPR statutes as well. In practice, the reasonable efforts provision is subject to a wide range of judicial interpretations. No clear judicial standard determines when efforts have been reasonable and when they have been too great or too cursory. Although some judicial variation is to be expected, the wide variation among these cases leads to delay in several ways.

Reluctant to spend precious time on legally risky cases, agency attorneys and social workers in many areas will prepare each case for a conservative interpretation. In these areas, petitions requesting termination of parental rights will be filed only when many services have been offered over a long period of time. To strengthen a case, services are sometimes offered whether the parent appears to benefit from them or not. When is enough, enough? The answer, in many areas, is "Not until we have a watertight case." This approach can cause damaging delays for children and unfairly prolong the issue with no benefit to parents.

Delays are also caused when attorneys for the agency decide not to take a case to TPR because of doubts about the technical interpretation of reasonable efforts. Have reasonable efforts been made when services were offered, but the parent didn't take advantage of them? Have reasonable efforts been made when the agency offered all available resources, but available resources were few and far between? What efforts are reasonable when a parent is due to be incarcerated for a long period of time?

Confusion and disagreement also surround the question of whether the reasonable efforts requirement should apply at all in deciding to terminate parental rights. What standard best protects the interests of the child at such a late stage in the case? State statutes vary, and judicial interpretations vary even more.

Lack of Legal Representation for the Agency

Some jurisdictions have no counsel assigned to represent the agency's position in permanency planning hearings. Sometimes this is true because a district attorney (D.A.) or prosecutor carries the case, representing the people of the state in general and not the agency's position as such. Conflicts may arise between the D.A.'s position and the agency's position. In jurisdictions that use the private attorney model (usually with state-employed assistant attorneys general), a shortage of attorneys in this role can cause a shortage of representation. In such cases, the attorney, usually brought in at the end of the process, has little basis on which to advise the social worker in the case preparation leading to the filing of a TPR petition.

Depriving the social worker of legal counsel can rule out fact-finding or service delivery activities that are important from the legal viewpoint but may not seem important to the social worker in serving the child. Waiting until late in the case to bring in an attorney can deprive that attorney of access to all the facts. A hastily convened conference in the hallway outside the courtroom can hardly pass for adequate legal counsel.

High Caseloads for Agency Social Workers, Defense Attorneys, and Attorneys Assigned to Represent the Agency

Cases are not getting the thorough professional attention they deserve due to pressures on professionals in all sectors of the system. Most practitioners confront daily contradictions between their own standards of best practice and what they are actually able to deliver under the constraints of high caseloads and short timelines. The lack of resources to provide adequate staffing is a problem in almost every jurisdiction studied.

Turnover in Professional Staff—Social Workers, Defense Attorneys, Assistant Attorneys General

Many child welfare agencies experience high turnover, as caseworkers are either reassigned or leave the field. It is not unusual for a child involved in a TPR hearing to have had four or five caseworkers. This is not true only for social workers, however. Systems of rotating juvenile court judges and high turnover in the attorney general and public defender offices are also commonplace. Delays in moving toward permanence are caused by changes in direction or information lost with the departure of the first caseworker, or delays while new relationships are established. Turnover leads to a shortage of professionals trained in dependency law and child welfare social work and causes delays while each new professional becomes familiar with the case or tries a new approach.

Differing Perspectives of Social Workers and Lawyers

Child welfare workers receive training in working with children and families in the setting of the child welfare agency, but little training in advocacy in the legal setting. More often than not, they are unschooled in adversarial methods and uneasy with this approach. Understandably, a social worker who has been trying to help a parent improve finds it difficult to change roles and speak against the parent's ability in a TPR hearing. The lawyer's logic and process orientation seem cold and passionless to the social worker. At the same time, lawyers may not understand the social worker's dilemmas or approaches and may feel frustration at the social worker's "emotionalism" or lack of appreciation for the rules of the court situation. One project coordinator remarked that watching members of the two professions try to collaborate was almost like watching attempts at communication between alien species.

Fragmentation of the System

Certain delays observed in all the projects could be attributed primarily to the logistics of communicating across agency and system boundaries. All the projects noted delays in passing along paperwork and necessary referral forms. The confidentiality requirements of medical and mental health professionals often pose obstacles to fact-finding. There is sometimes a lack of clarity or a difference of opinion regarding the role each party plays in achieving permanence for a child. The role of advocates, such as court appointed special advocates, guardians ad litem, and citizen review boards, is often unclear, as these groups have arrived on the scene relatively recently. What information to transmit and how to transmit information are not always clear.

Docketing and Scheduling Problems

Across the country, dependency cases compete with criminal and civil cases for time on the dockets of crowded court systems. There are so many parties to a typical case that it is difficult to reconvene them all when hearings extend beyond the allocated number of days. Continuances—in some jurisdictions routinely requested by the defense and granted by judges—delay cases for months with no change in the facts of the case. When a criminal prosecution of one of the parents is pending, as in cases where sexual abuse is alleged, the dependency proceedings are sometimes put on hold. Judges complain that much time is spent in hearing uncontested facts.

Appeals

In some states, all TPR cases are automatically appealed. Depending on how many layers of court systems are available, an appeal can add up to three years to a case—three years of uncertainty for the child.

Proliferation of Review Hearings and Inefficient Use of Judicial Hearings

Some jurisdictions report a proliferation of case review systems for monitoring the agencies' progress with each case and for providing community oversight and input into child welfare cases. In some jurisdictions, each of these reviews and hearings calls for different documentation from caseworkers. Caseworkers and attorneys alike complain that time spent preparing for and attending case reviews and court hearings means less time to work with children and families.

Casework Practice Issues

Sketchy information collection at intake leads to surprises later, or to placement decisions that slow the case down. Information often missed includes status under the Indian Child Welfare Act of 1978 (ICWA), in the case of Native American children, and the names and addresses of putative fathers and members of the extended family or other significant adults.

When case planning progresses, it often fails to meet professional standards. So-called standardized service plans may have nothing to do with the parents' primary problems, may not promote reunification, and may easily be challenged by defense attorneys in TPR hearings. Clear timelines for parental improvement with clear consequences for lack of progress are routinely missing. Parents may not be clear about how they have to change in order to reunify their families. This lack of clarity is obviously an obstacle to reunification. It may also delay the granting of TPR later in the case.

As a consequence of poor child welfare casework, children wait while social workers go back to find fathers or identify other relatives. If a child who has been with the agency for several years is discovered to have Indian status, all service delivery and placement decisions up to that point are called into question, because Indian Child Welfare Advisory Committees have not been involved. A child may have been placed with, and become bonded to, an unrelated foster parent when relatives were available as a permanent resource. Resolving these dilemmas is heart-wrenching and challenging to the children, communities, and professionals involved.

The same practice improvements that would help release a child for timely adoption would also promote timely reunification. In fact, assertive TPR casework often uncovers situations in which families can be reunified.

Lack of Treatment and Placement Resources

What should constitute reasonable efforts when treatment resources are limited or nonexistent? For example, many communities have waiting lists for drug treatment facilities, lack transportation to services, or lack culturally appropriate parenting classes. Foster homes may not be near to parents, so visiting necessary to maintain bonding is hampered. There may be no effective services for parents who are incarcerated. Under such conditions, it is obviously hard to prove that reasonable efforts have been made. In the absence of pertinent resources, professionals are reluctant to file TPR petitions, and case resolution is delayed.

Children with Special Needs

What is the best way to secure legal permanence for children who are institutionalized? For teenagers? For children for whom no adoptive home is available? Are the trauma and expense of a TPR hearing advisable in the range of special cases where an adoptive home may not be found for the child? Will aggressive pursuit of termination of parental rights force the system to step up to bat and find permanent family ties for each child in the system? These questions are sometimes resolved more with an eye to efficiency than with an eye to permanence for children.

Special Parental Circumstances

Parental circumstances such as incarceration, drug addiction, chronic mental illness, and severe developmental disabilities present a challenge to reunification efforts. What efforts are reasonable to support reunification with a parent in such circumstances? Are appropriate services available? At what cost? Some advocates complain that caseworkers act too conservatively in such cases, providing services beyond the point where benefits are likely, just to build a watertight case. Yet evidence suggests that much can be done for parents with these problems if resources and skills are adequate and extended families are involved.

Practice Delays with Children of Color

Children of color remain in care longer and in less appropriate placements than the majority of Caucasian children placed by the same agencies. Special efforts and a legal framework were established for Indian children under the Indian Child Welfare Act of 1978. Still, for Native American children as well as other minorities, agencies have not recruited enough foster homes, and culturally appropriate services are scarce. Homes that would be appropriate from a cultural point of view may be ruled out by agency licensing procedures. Kinship care placements and the support of extended family members, often the best resources, especially in minority communities, are not always used effectively. Caseworkers lack training in identifying and screening relatives. Language barriers between client families and caseworkers or attorneys cause delays at all points in the process.

Successful Approaches

Research findings are consistent from state to state and across the family and child welfare continuum. The same problems that delay adoption for children for whom it would be appropriate also delay reunification for children whose families have workable strengths.

Certain significant and worthwhile improvements have been made, however, by each of the four federally funded projects. These improvements are within the reach of lawyers, agency administrators, and caseworkers. They can be brought about by changes in statute and administrative law, by training and cross-training of personnel, and by implementing improved practice protocols. The results in these projects were produced by changes in four categories.

Legal and Administrative Changes

Changes in law and policy to improve the framework for decision making are best demonstrated by the Michigan experience, where state timelines now move cases along to decision sooner than is required by federal laws. Most of the projects also altered court and administrative practice rules and state statutes setting grounds for termination of parental rights.

Practice Changes for Social Workers and Lawyers

All four project reports discuss ways to improve casework and legal professional practice, promoting necessary changes by means of training and increased support from supervisors and consultants. In particular, all the projects emphasized better information-gathering by the agency during the initial investigation, especially in finding out about fathers, extended families and other natural support systems, and ICWA status. Attention to cultural and ethnic considerations can improve placement decisions and prevent delays in reunification or release for adoption. Also identified across the board was the importance of accurately assessing the problems that put the child at risk.

Agency social workers need greater support from trained legal counsel. Ideally, agency counsel should be available early in the planning of each case to give advice and to clarify the roles of all parties.

Timelines must be enforced rigorously, monitoring progress and establishing clear consequences for failure to comply. Compliance with the case plan within set timelines must be required of everyone, not just parents.

Improved Interagency Collaboration

Strategies to promote interagency collaboration are essential. Examples include administrative-level task forces, cross-training, role clarification, and case conferences that include attorneys, social workers, and other parties. Professionals in all settings need training on how to work effectively with others.

Outcomes for cases and for system improvements must be clearly defined. Data that demonstrate progress toward these goals must be collected and shared among agencies. A clear common view of progress and problems can move agencies into better collaborative relationships.

Funding Changes

Increasing staff and decreasing caseload sizes brings about marked improvements in the timeliness of permanency planning, as noted in several states when staff members were added at bottlenecks in the system. For example, adding assistant attorneys general and adding social workers correlated directly with more children becoming legally free for adoption. Increasing treatment resources for parents, such as drug treatment facilities, was a prerequisite for reducing delays. Collaboration among agencies to share case costs and clarify treatment priorities also reduced some of the delays.

Conclusion

The following pages illuminate four different approaches to reducing delays for children in foster care. Professionals at many points in the system will find suggestions for changes they can make to enhance and expedite decision-making so that children can return home or find another permanent family in a timely way.

CHAPTER 2

The Michigan Agency Attorney Project

David Herring

This chapter is a major product of a federal grant project conducted by the Child Advocacy Law Clinic at the University of Michigan Law School. The project sought to reduce significantly the amount of time a child typically spends in temporary foster care before the social welfare agency makes a permanency decision, defined by the project as the agency's decision concerning the appropriate permanent family home for a child in temporary foster care. Permanency decisions could include a return to the parental home, a termination of parental rights (TPR) and a permanent adoptive placement, or, when appropriate, a long-term family foster care placement. Since obtaining a timely permanency decision from the Michigan courts is assured in most cases once the agency has made its decision, the project focused on the time period from the initial report of suspected abuse or neglect to the date of the agency's permanency decision. The flowchart on the next page illustrates the strict time requirements for court procedures in Michigan.

The project hoped to achieve timely agency permanency decisions by improving the legal representation provided to the social welfare agency in civil child protection cases. The project's hypothesis was that many delays could be reduced significantly by employing a private model of legal representation rather than the public model currently used in most jurisdictions. The two models are described below.

Flowchart for Child Abuse and Neglect Cases under Michigan Law*

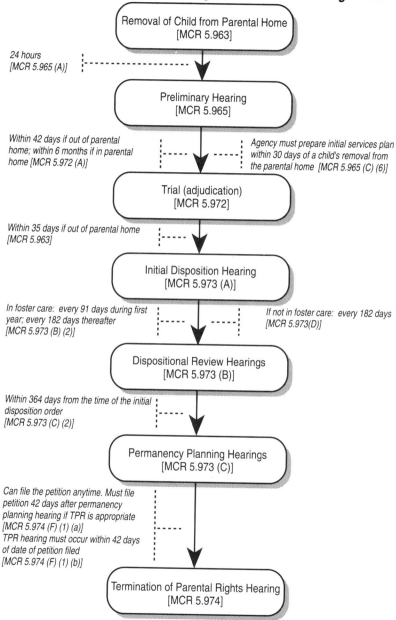

Removal of Child from Parental Home
[MCR 5.963]

*24 hours
[MCR 5.965 (A)]*

Preliminary Hearing
[MCR 5.965]

*Within 42 days if out of parental
home; within 6 months if in parental
home [MCR 5.972 (A)]*

*Agency must prepare initial services plan
within 30 days of a child's removal from
the parental home [MCR 5.965 (C) (6)]*

Trial (adjudication)
[MCR 5.972]

*Within 35 days if out of parental home
[MCR 5.963]*

Initial Disposition Hearing
[MCR 5.973 (A)]

*In foster care: every 91 days during first
year; every 182 days thereafter
[MCR 5.973 (B) (2)]*

*If not in foster care: every 182 days
[MCR 5.973(D)]*

Dispositional Review Hearings
[MCR 5.973 (B)]

*Within 364 days from the time of the initial
disposition order
[MCR 5.973 (C) (2)]*

Permanency Planning Hearings
[MCR 5.973 (C)]

*Can file the petition anytime. Must file
petition 42 days after permanency
planning hearing if TPR is appropriate
[MCR 5.974 (F) (1) (a)]
TPR hearing must occur within 42 days
of date of petition filed
[MCR 5.974 (F) (1) (b)]*

Termination of Parental Rights Hearing
[MCR 5.974]

* Citations are to Michigan Court Rules

This project arose from observations of the public model of legal representation made by the law students and the supervising attorneys in the Child Advocacy Law Clinic at the University of Michigan Law School. In the clinic, law students working in teams of two represented children, parents, or the Michigan Department of Social Services (DSS) in child abuse and neglect matters. The students represented children in one county (Genesee) and parents in another county (Oakland) from the very start of legal proceedings. In six counties (including the four counties where the project was conducted), the students represented DSS in cases in which the agency had decided to seek termination of parental rights. In the TPR cases where they represented DSS, the students usually became involved in a case long after it entered the courts; they would draft a petition seeking TPR and then represent DSS at the hearing.

Attorneys supervising students in the clinic were disturbed at the substantial harm being inflicted on children by the drawn-out proceedings that were common in the most serious cases of child abuse and neglect. Experts agree that a child needs a permanent, stable family home environment in order to develop in a healthy and normal way.[1] Although more research must be done, it is clear that a child may suffer substantial developmental harm if placed in the emotional limbo of temporary foster care for an extended period of time.[2] The risk of substantial developmental harm resulting from lengthy temporary foster care placements constitutes the basis for the federal law requirement that "reasonable efforts" be made to prevent or shorten out-of-home placements and the requirement that courts attempt to make permanent decisions for children within 18 months after they are removed from their homes.[3]

Despite the undisputed conclusions from the fields of social work, psychology, psychiatry, and pediatrics concerning a child's need for timely permanency, DSS was not initiating TPR cases until children had been in temporary foster care for anywhere from two to 10 years. Two years in temporary foster care is a long time for a young child, and can often result in substantial harm to the child.[4] The harm resulting from extended temporary foster care placement may actually be worse for the child than the abuse or neglect originally suffered in the parental home.[5]

The clinic faculty also observed many examples of delayed court proceedings. Many of these delays were directly or indirectly attributable to the legal representation provided to DSS by the local prosecutors' offices. In the majority of cases, a prosecutor would appear only at the initial trial, and, if the DSS on its own initiative sought TPR, at the subsequent TPR hearing. At all other hearings, such as preliminary hearings, dispositional hearings, and periodic review hearings, the DSS social worker was not represented by an attorney in court. DSS social workers, often uncomfortable with the adversarial nature of the court process and unfamiliar with the statutes and court rules requiring timely procedures in child abuse and neglect cases, were frequently forced or persuaded to accept delays and adjournments that accommodated the court's or opposing counsels' schedule and agenda, but were not in a child's best interest.

Beyond the failure of local prosecutors to appear at court hearings, a lack of active legal consultation for DSS was also observed. Even at trial and TPR hearings, it was often obvious that the prosecutor had not talked to the DSS social worker or looked at the case file before the day of the court proceeding. The social worker was left alone to set case goals and even to achieve them in court. The prosecutors were not taking an active role in planning permanence for children, or setting a solid legal foundation for later TPR proceedings, should these become necessary.

In fact, in some cases, the prosecutor actually undermined the social worker's position. This happened in two ways: first, prosecutors would sometimes refuse to allow the filing or pursuit of petitions that they felt were too difficult to prove; and second, prosecutors were often willing to negotiate with opposing counsel by striking portions of the petition in return for a no-contest plea, which eliminated the need for a trial. These amendments to the petition were sometimes made over the objections of the social worker and without considering the effect such amendments could later have on achieving permanence for a child or effective treatment for a parent. For example, if the petition were amended in a way that obscured parental problems and hid them from the court, an effective family reunification plan would not be ordered at the subsequent dispositional hearing. The opportunity for a timely permanent return of the child to the parental home could therefore be lost or significantly delayed. If the petition was amended to remove the most serious allegations of abuse or neglect, the chance to later achieve TPR on the basis of the parents' original problems could also be lost.[6]

The Project's Methodology

This project involved the four counties of Jackson, Calhoun, Livingston, and Monroe. The project's staff attorney, applying the private model of legal representation, represented the DSS in half of the child abuse and neglect cases filed in the pertinent courts between April 1, 1989, and December 31, 1989. The local county prosecutors continued to represent DSS in the other half of the child abuse and neglect cases filed in the same period. The research assistant collected detailed information on each case at each stage in the proceedings (preliminary hearing, pretrial, trial, initial dispositional hearing, dispositional review hearings, permanency hearing, and TPR hearing). This information has allowed the project staff to begin a detailed comparison of case results achieved by the private and public models of legal representation.

Information was also collected on cases filed between January 1, 1987, and June 30, 1987, because Michigan law concerning child abuse and neglect matters changed substantially when new legislation went into effect on April 1, 1989. By April 1, 1989, all the 1987 cases should have run their course under the previous Michigan law. Comparing the data on these 1987 cases and the project's 1989 cases made it possible to identify changes in case results attributable to the change in the law.

In addition to the report embodied in this chapter, a training manual for attorneys representing the agency was also completed, in April 1991. The results of a detailed statistical analysis of project data, completed in 1992, were published in the *Toledo Law Review*, volume 24, number 3. A fuller discussion of the products of the project concludes this chapter.

The Public Model of Legal Representation

Many reasons lay behind the lack of effective legal representation being provided to DSS. First, the county prosecutors' offices operate on limited resources, most of which are allocated to criminal prosecutions. The county prosecutors provide legal representation to DSS, but DSS does not pay for these legal services or participate in the selection of the assistant prosecutor assigned to each case. Because civil child protection cases are seldom a top priority of local prosecutors, and because they receive no additional state funds for this service, there is no incentive for thorough, active advocacy.

The attitude and training level of some assistant prosecutors assigned to the juvenile court compound the problem of limited resources. Juvenile court is usually the first assignment an assistant prosecutor receives, because the stakes in a civil proceeding are considered low compared to those in a criminal proceeding. Effectively, then, the juvenile court becomes a training ground for inexperienced assistant prosecutors, many of whom feel that they are only assigned to the juvenile court for the time it takes to learn the basics of trial practice (usually one year) before they can move on to the meatier adult criminal court assignments. DSS is therefore often represented by inexperienced attorneys who are not particularly interested in the issues and procedures surrounding civil child protection proceedings.

County prosecutors also have difficulty adjusting to representing an agency such as DSS. This may be due in large part to the prosecutor's usual role of representing the people of the state at large. Most prosecutors feel that this public model of legal representation applies in the area of civil child protection proceedings as well. Under the public model of legal representation, DSS social workers are not perceived as clients who are the ultimate decision makers and entitled to active, zealous legal representation. Instead, the workers are often viewed merely as witnesses or investigating officers. As a result, the prosecutors apply their own view of what is in the interest of the people of the state, and feel free to veto the decisions made by DSS social workers.

The Private Model of Legal Representation: The Agency Attorney Project

The Attorney-Client Relationship

The project hypothesized that permanency for children could be achieved most effectively under an alternative to the public model of legal representation for DSS. The project attorney proposed to represent DSS using a private model of legal representation, adhering to the rules and ethics that apply in the usual private attorney-client relationship. The attorney would view the agency as the client and the social worker as the representative of the agency. The social worker would be entitled to zealous advocacy by the attorney. Although the attorney would make decisions concerning legal procedures and strategies and would advise the worker on these decisions, the social worker, as client representative, would make the ultimate, substantive decisions in the case on the basis of social work considerations.[7]

The project attorney believed that the philosophy of legal representation embodied in the private model would make a significant difference in achieving timely permanency decisions for children. As a zealous advocate for the agency, the attorney was available at all times for legal consultation with the social worker client representatives. The attorney encouraged social workers to call for legal advice before they filed a petition with the court. The attorney could then counsel the social worker on the appropriateness of filing a petition and of removing a child from the parental home; assist in drafting a detailed initial petition to lay the necessary foundation for later stages in the case, such as disposition and possible return home or TPR; and could, from day one, begin to develop the strong attorney-client team relationship that is the ideal in the private model of legal representation.

Also from the very beginning of the case, the project attorney made it clear that she would pursue the social worker's goals in the case. The attorney would provide consultation on legal issues and other matters, but the social worker was made fully aware that he or she determined the ultimate case goals, such as seeking court jurisdiction, removing a child from the parental home, providing services for family reunification, returning a child home, dismissing the case from court, or seeking TPR.

The attorney also made it clear that she would be present at all court hearings, accompanying the social worker to the preliminary hearing, the pretrial and trial, the initial dispositional hearing, the dispositional review hearings, the permanency hearing, and the TPR hearing. Social workers who, when appearing in court alone, had often been intimidated by opposing counsel into yielding on certain points of their case plan were assured of the constant presence of their own attorney.

This team model of advocacy in court would provide protection for the integrity of a social worker's professionally developed case plan. In addition, throughout the case, the attorney would consult with social workers outside of court. First, before important court appearances, the attorney would meet with the social worker and any other witnesses to fully prepare them to testify in court. But most importantly, the project attorney would meet with the social worker to discuss and set the case goals that would achieve permanence for the child involved in the case. Strong attorney support in early consultations and at subsequent court hearings would allow a close attorney-social worker team relationship to develop.

The attorney would therefore be in a good position to help the social worker achieve an agency permanency decision in the case as early as possible, pressing for a timely decision as a zealous, supportive advocate. The substance of the decision would be left to the social worker, but the attorney's goal would be to obtain a permanency decision from the worker within one year from the time a child was removed from the parental home. The social worker would not be left alone to come to a permanency decision at some indefinite time in the future.[8]

The project focused on the time period leading to the agency's permanency decision because this approach was appropriate under Michigan law. Once the agency makes the decision—to return the child to the parental home, seek TPR, or recommend long-term family foster care—implementing the decision in court does not create significant delays. The Michigan courts, pursuant to the Michigan Court Rules (MCR), must hold review hearings every three months during the first year a child is placed out of the home.[9] It is relatively easy to present the court with the agency's permanency decision. If the agency decides, for example, to file a TPR petition, the TPR court hearing must take place within 42 days and the court's decision must be entered within 28 days after the hearing.[10] These time limits, if honored by the courts, facilitate and encourage prompt implementation of the permanency goal once the DSS has made its decision. In our experience, these statutes and court rules, which became effective on April 1, 1989, are being implemented in good faith, and have reduced any significant delays following the formulation of a permanency decision by the agency. Again, see figure 1, a flowchart of a civil child protection proceeding under current Michigan law.

In some states, however, the period between agency permanency decision and judicial action is subject to substantial delays. The other projects described in this book have explored creative methods beyond legislative and court rule reform to deal with these time lags.

Interdisciplinary Training

What the Attorney Needs to Know

To properly implement the private model of legal representation in child abuse and neglect cases, the project attorney received training in disciplines other than the law. This training was necessary to communicate effectively with the social workers and to gain insight before counseling them on developing and implementing case plans. Through readings and lectures in psychiatry, social work, and pediatrics, the attorney learned about basic concepts of child development, causes of abuse and neglect, mental and physical symptoms of abuse and neglect, a child's need for a permanent family home, and services available to deal with family problems leading to abuse and neglect. (See the reading list that follows this chapter for a sample of the attorney's interdisciplinary readings.)

Beyond these general concepts, the attorney learned from social workers and other professionals in each of the four project counties about the resources available in these communities for treating parents and children, such as substance abuse evaluation and treatment, mental health evaluation and counseling, and intensive in-home assistance to prevent removal of the child from the parental home.

The importance of this interdisciplinary training cannot be overemphasized. The agency attorney must have a background in child welfare to be able to provide the counseling, support, and zealous advocacy required by the private model of legal representation. The attorney must speak the language of the social worker and must have the knowledge required to assist in developing and assessing the social worker's case plan. The attorney must know what services are effective and available in the particular community to help reunify a dysfunctional family. Only with this knowledge can the attorney identify cases where the social worker should currently be reaching a permanency decision, and then help her or him to make a timely decision.

This interdisciplinary training is necessary even to understand child abuse and neglect legislation. For example, the current Michigan law is an implementation of the concepts of effective permanency planning for children. Michigan law now sets out time requirements for each hearing and directs the court to conduct a permanency hearing one year after an initial disposition order placing a child outside the parental home. To fully understand and implement this law in individual cases, the agency attorney must know why it is important for children to have a permanent home and when they need such a home. The attorney also must be aware of the damage that can be done to children by disrupting their previously permanent parental home, even if that home presents some risk to a child.

Training is also essential for the agency attorney to participate effectively in periodic social worker case conferences, which may include professionals from other relevant disciplines such as psychiatry, psychology, and medicine. The attorney must be able to operate beyond the role of a legal mechanic to get the social workers and other professionals to come to concrete case plan recommendations and to address permanency planning issues from the very beginning of a case. The training enables the agency attorney to realize that attendance and full participation at social work and multidisciplinary case conferences are vital.

What the Social Worker Needs to Know

For the attorney-social worker team to function effectively, the social worker must acquire a basic knowledge of the substantive and procedural law that applies to child protection proceedings. The Michigan project attorney conducted training sessions for the social workers, emphasizing the need for the social workers to begin every case with a permanency perspective.

These sessions included discussions on the community-specific definition of reasonable efforts to avoid removing a child from the parental home, but more importantly, they included detailed discussions on the need for written case plans that document the social worker's permanency planning decision-making process from the beginning of each case. The attorney emphasized that documentation was necessary in every case—to support a subsequent request for reunification of the family, for TPR, or for long-term family foster care. Sessions included discussion of the procedural timing requirements of the Michigan statutes and court rules. The attorney outlined the entire court process in child protection proceedings and explained what the court would expect at each stage.

The sessions also served as an especially effective way to begin the attorney-social worker team relationship. The social workers expressed many fears of the court process (especially fears of judges and opposing counsel) and many frustrations with the legal representation provided by the local prosecutors' offices.

By explaining the private model of legal representation, the attorney assured the social workers that she was their attorney, available for consultation and advice on how to proceed, and at times would push them for a permanency decision, although they controlled the substantive case decisions. She assured them that she would zealously advocate for their decisions in court, that she would attend every court hearing and deal with opposing counsel, and that she would prepare them to testify before court appearances and would also protect them when they were being cross-examined in court.

The Crucial Importance of Cross-Training

In sum, it is crucial for implementation of the private model of legal representation that both the attorney and the social worker understand the issues that each faces in their common cases. Only in this way can the agency attorney effectively counsel, advise, and push the social worker on necessary case decisions. And only in this way can the social worker provide the effective day-to-day services and documentation the attorney needs to achieve favorable court decisions. The early integration of knowledge and effort allows the attorney-social worker team to present a logical, coherent case plan to the court and to achieve timely permanency decisions for children.

Overview of the Michigan Child Abuse and Neglect Law

Since the project was conducted in four Michigan counties, the Michigan statutes and court rules applicable in child abuse and neglect matters formed the legal setting for the project's cases. These statutes and court rules became effective on April 1, 1989, the day the project attorney began representing agency social workers in court, and offered a very favorable legal environment for implementing the private model of legal representation and for achieving timely permanency decisions for children. This section describes the important procedural aspects of the statutory and court rule scheme that supported the goals of the private model.

Time Requirements for Court Procedures

The time requirements for each stage of the court process are a major component of the statutes and court rules. Initially, the court must open a preliminary hearing within 24 hours after a child is removed from the parental home. The preliminary hearing may be conducted in the parents' absence if proper notice has been given to the parents. The court can only adjourn the preliminary hearing for up to 14 days to secure the attendance of witnesses or for other good cause shown. The court must instruct the agency to prepare an initial case service plan within 30 days from the date of the child's removal from the home.

Following a preliminary hearing in which the court authorizes continued placement of the child outside the parental home, the court must hold a trial within 42 days. (After the project, this period was extended to 63 days.) The trial can be postponed only if

- all the parties, including the agency, agree to a postponement;
- service of process cannot be completed (very unusual since service by publication is expressly allowed); or
- the court finds that the testimony of a presently unavailable witness is needed (also very unusual).

The attorney for this project refused to stipulate to any postponements beyond the 42-day period. When a trial is postponed for either of the last two reasons, the court must release the child to the parent unless the court finds that returning the child to the parent's custody will likely result in physical harm or serious emotional damage to the child. This is a significant incentive for the court to avoid adjournments beyond the 42-day period.

Once the trial has been completed, the court must conduct the initial dispositional hearing within 35 days. In the vast majority of cases, the initial dispositional hearing is conducted on the same day, immediately after the trial. The dispositional hearing may take place without the respondent parents being present if they have been given proper notice, either through service of process or by scheduling the hearing on the record at trial in the presence of the parties. The agency must prepare a written case report and case service plan that will be available to all parties prior to the initial dispositional hearing. (The case report and case service plan are usually made available the day before the hearing or the day of the hearing.)

Following the initial dispositional hearing, the court must conduct dispositional review hearings every 91 days during the first year a child is placed outside the parental home. The agency must submit a revised case plan to the court every 90 days if the child remains in out-of-home care. This procedure is designed to provide intensive agency and court involvement in, and review of, cases during the first year of removal. Review hearings can be held before the required date if swift progress toward reunification or other permanent resolution of the case is foreseen. After the first year, the court must conduct review hearings every 182 days.

If the child remains in an out-of-home placement and parental rights have not been terminated, the court must hold a permanency hearing not more than 364 days from the time of the initial dispositional hearing. See below for a full discussion of the permanency hearing.

Under Michigan law, termination of parental rights can be sought at the initial dispositional hearing or at any time thereafter. TPR must be requested in the original petition or in an amended or supplemental petition. The request for TPR can be made by the prosecutor, the agency, or the representative of the child. The TPR hearing must be conducted no later than 42 days after a supplemental petition seeking TPR has been filed. The 42-day period may be extended "for good cause shown," but only for an additional 21 days. This 42-day rule has been extremely effective in motivating courts to conduct timely TPR proceedings. The court must file its decision on TPR within 28 days after a TPR hearing has been completed.

The statutory grounds for TPR are spelled out in Michigan Compiled Laws (MCL) 712A.19b(3)(a)-(i). The most important statutory grounds include desertion of a child for 91 or more days; physical abuse that is likely to recur in the foreseeable future if the child is placed in the parental home (this includes a parent's failure to protect a child from physical abuse); the failure of a parent, for a period in excess of 182 days, to rectify the conditions that led to removal of the child from the parental home when there is no reasonable likelihood that the conditions will be rectified within a reasonable time, considering the age of the child;

the parent's long-term neglect of the child that will continue into the foreseeable future, without regard to the intent or blameworthiness of the parent; imprisonment of a parent for a period in excess of two years that will deprive the child of a normal home; and a previous decision to terminate parental rights in regard to a sibling, when previous attempts to rehabilitate the parents have been unsuccessful.

If a court does enter an order of TPR and the child remains in foster care, review hearings are conducted every 182 days thereafter. At these review hearings, the court monitors the agency's progress in obtaining a permanent placement for the child. At this stage, the agency attorney needs to follow through with the social worker to ensure that an adoptive placement or other permanent placement is found for the child.

The time requirements spelled out in the applicable statutes and court rules have been a mainstay of the project attorney's efforts to achieve timely permanency decisions for children. The attorney, thoroughly preparing for court hearings with the social worker, has, in the vast majority of cases, been able to avoid adjournments beyond the time periods spelled out in the statutes and court rules. The attorney has given the courts no excuse for not proceeding appropriately, and has, in fact, vigorously opposed any unnecessary delays. With this type of zealous advocacy, the courts have faithfully implemented the statutory and court rule time requirements in almost all the project cases. This legal framework has enabled the agency to achieve timely permanency decisions for children within its care.

The Permanency Hearing

The federal law governing federal payments for foster care and adoption assistance, PL 96-272, requires the court to consider permanency planning issues no later then 18 months after a child is originally placed in foster care. Michigan law adopts and strengthens this requirement in the child abuse and neglect legislation that went into effect in April 1989 by creating a special hearing, called the permanency hearing, which must be conducted within a year of the original out-of-home placement. More than any other single provision of the new Michigan law, this provision reveals the philosophy and reasoning that form the basis of the legislation. It is grounded in the concept of timely permanency planning for children that arises from the integrated disciplines of social work and child development psychology.

The provisions of the permanency hearing provide the driving force behind the private model of legal representation. The project was designed to fully implement the 1989 Michigan legislation by means of an active agency attorney-social worker team. The permanency hearing stage is the point in each case at which the benefits to the social worker and the child derived from the private model of legal representation are most pronounced.

Even in states with no express provision for a permanency hearing, the Michigan permanency hearing concepts can serve as a best-practice model. The agency attorney can adopt the requirements and suggestions discussed below as guidelines or recommendations. Generally, the attorney should aim from the beginning of a case to treat the review hearing that will take place one year after the child is removed from the parental home as a permanency hearing. An agency attorney in a jurisdiction without an express permanency hearing provision can achieve the same result by working closely with the social worker client from the beginning of each case.

To achieve timely permanence in the absence of an express permanency planning provision, the agency attorney will have to discuss the issue with the individual social workers and reach agreement that a timely permanency decision is vital to the healthy development of a child. The attorney must focus the worker on decision-making based on good social work practice and assure the worker that she or he will advocate strongly for the worker's permanency decision, whether it is return to the parental home, TPR, or guardianship.

The attorney should help the social worker feel confident enough to make sound, timely permanency decisions and to work with the attorney to achieve those decisions in court. For his or her part, the social worker must provide and document proper social work services and make social work decisions in a time frame that achieves the permanency needs of each particular child.

Because the Michigan law so clearly describes the decisions the court must make at a permanency hearing, it is presented here as a model of the decisions an agency attorney in any jurisdiction should urge the social worker to make within one year of a child's removal. The Michigan law requires the court to conduct a permanency hearing for a child who has remained in family foster care since the court's initial disposition order. The court must conduct the permanency hearing not more than 364 days after entry of its initial disposition order, and may combine the permanency hearing with a dispositional review hearing. Thus, the fourth three-month review hearing usually becomes the permanency hearing.

The express purpose of the permanency hearing is to review the status of the child and the progress being made toward the child's return home, or to show why the child should not be placed in the permanent custody of the court. This rather general statement of purpose is supported by a protocol of decisions the court must make at the permanency hearing. The court has four options.

Return Home

First, if TPR has not been ordered and the court determines that returning the child to the parental home would not cause a substantial risk of harm to the child's life, physical health, or mental well-being, the court must order the child returned to the parental home. This first priority is a permanency decision for the child: return to the parental home.

Initiation of TPR Proceedings

The court's second option is a finding that the child would face a substantial risk of harm in the parental home and therefore should not be returned home. If the court makes such a finding, the social welfare agency must initiate TPR proceedings by filing a petition seeking TPR within 42 days after the permanency hearing, unless it can demonstrate to the court that TPR is clearly not in the child's best interests. This second-priority option is again a permanency decision for the child: seek TPR and adoption.

If the court finds that the child cannot be returned to the parental home *and* the agency demonstrates that TPR is clearly not in the best interests of the child, the court has two additional alternatives. If the court determines that it is in the child's best interests, the court can order that the child be placed in foster care on a long-term basis. If the court determines that a permanent placement is not possible, it can order the continuation of the child's temporary foster care placement for a limited period to be expressly stated by the court.

Long-Term Foster Care

The first of these last alternatives effectively results in a permanency decision for the child: a long-term family foster care placement. In some cases, long-term placement in a stable foster home is the best available permanency decision. The major problem with long-term foster care placements is the risk of a subsequent change in placement and the resulting risk of harm to the child.[11] However, safeguards can be constructed to reduce these risks.

For example, in project cases where long-term foster care was the agency's permanency decision, the foster parents were asked to sign a family foster care agreement that clearly stated the long-term nature of the placement. In addition, the attorney requested the court to include the long-term family foster care agreement in the court order. A degree of formality was therefore accorded to the agreement, bringing home to the foster parents the commitment they were making and reducing the risk of later disruption of the placement. In many cases, this type of permanent placement fulfills the need of the child for a permanent, stable home.

Temporary Foster Care

Continuing temporary foster care is much more troublesome in terms of achieving a timely permanency decision for the child. It allows the agency and the court to avoid making a permanency decision by continuing the child's placement in temporary foster care for a stated period of time—usually six months, because after the first year, review hearings are required only every six months. The child is starting down the road to spending a substantial period of time in a temporary foster care placement.

In some unusual cases, continuing a temporary foster care placement beyond one year is appropriate, as, for example, when the parent is an adequate parent but will not be released from prison for another six months. In most cases, however, a continued temporary foster care placement is inappropriate because it fails to meet the child's need for a timely permanent resolution. In the vast majority of cases, the agency and the courts should avoid the "escape hatch" option that allows continuation of a temporary foster care placement beyond one year.

The project attorney played a key role in avoiding the temptation to take advantage of this last alternative, having witnessed the court's use of the option in many cases handled by local prosecutors. In those cases, the agency social worker would come to the permanency hearing without having made a permanency decision in the case. In court, the social worker or the prosecutor (if he or she was present) would merely request more time to work with the family. The court—without much of a challenge in most cases—would then order a continuation of the temporary foster care placement for a period of three to six months.

The project attorney, however, worked closely with the social worker from the beginning of each case to reach a permanency decision within the one-year period. In most of the project cases, the social worker made a permanency decision before the case even got to the permanency hearing stage, and in virtually all the project cases, the social worker made a decision by the time of the permanency hearing. Thus, the agency attorney did not request the court to continue temporary family foster care placements, and the court did not use this option in project cases.

In the project cases, the social worker and the court implemented the Michigan permanency planning law in good faith and made timely permanency decisions for children. The result was to avoid substantial time spent in foster care drift for children in project cases.

Implications for Other States

As discussed above, effective permanency planning may often have to be done without the assistance of a statute such as Michigan's, which expressly requires the court to address permanency issues. The agency attorney can still have a substantial impact in working within a system to obtain timely permanency decisions for children. The Michigan statute provides a solid framework that can be applied by an agency attorney in any jurisdiction to incorporate permanency considerations from the very beginning of a child abuse or neglect case and to achieve timely, permanent results for children.

However, since the Michigan statute requiring permanency hearings provides the agency attorney with such a powerful tool, agency attorneys in other jurisdictions should strongly consider making legislative and court rule reform efforts that would incorporate permanency planning concepts. Beyond individual case advocacy, the agency attorney should take time to consider broad policy reforms that would assist the agency in permanency planning. The agency attorney should take on the role of policy advocate, approaching officials in the offices of the state attorney general, state legislators, and the state supreme court to pursue legislative and court rule reforms, and should actively participate in drafting new legislation and court rules and in lobbying for their adoption.

Specific Issues around Termination of Parental Rights Proceedings

Preparation for the TPR Hearing

From day one of a case, the agency attorney and the agency social worker must keep in mind the possibility of eventually seeking termination of parental rights. They must be sure that if TPR becomes the permanent plan for the child, they will be able to establish the necessary statutory grounds at the TPR hearing. To do this, they have to work together to formulate a logical case plan that effectively deals with the family's actual problems. The attorney must see that the social worker fully documents, first, the parents' compliance in visiting or communicating with the child and following through with services, then the parents' family history, including previous agency or court involvement, the term of incarceration for any imprisoned parent, and so on. Complete case planning and documentation were major components of the project attorney's case-by-case guidance.

The failure of the agency attorney and the social worker to prepare for TPR from the beginning of a case can often cause unnecessary, harmful delays in achieving TPR. This is true even in Michigan where there are clear time requirements for court procedures. A court can easily avoid the time requirement if it feels the case must be developed further in order to reach a decision.

For example, as stated above, the court must file its TPR decision within 28 days after a TPR hearing has been completed. One judge in the project counties, however, would sometimes adjourn TPR hearings for up to six months before all the evidence had been presented, thus effectively delaying his decision beyond the 28-day period. This judge created these delays to give parents one more chance to rehabilitate themselves, under his own intensive case plan. The judge, in effect, stepped into the role of social worker.

These delays were avoided in project cases by having the project attorney and the social worker develop a very intensive case plan from the beginning of each case, so that if parents were unable to make the necessary changes, this could be established by clear and convincing evidence presented at the initial TPR hearing. Only on clear evidence would this judge complete the TPR hearing in a timely manner and reach a decision within the required 28-day period. The agency attorney and the social worker must work together from the very beginning of a case if subsequent harmful delays in achieving permanency decisions for children are to be avoided.

The Reasonable Efforts Requirement and Termination of Parental Rights

Some states, such as New York, include within their statutory grounds for TPR a requirement that the agency prove it has made "reasonable" or "diligent" efforts to reunite the family. As far as the agency and the child are concerned, including such a requirement in the statutory grounds for TPR is ill-advised. The law asks for a finding concerning the agency's reasonable efforts to reunite the family in order for the agency to obtain federal funding for the state's temporary foster care placement system. Under federal law, this determination of whether or not the agency has made reasonable efforts is relevant at court proceedings only when the agency is seeking to continue the child's temporary family foster care placement—at the initial disposition hearing or the periodic review hearings. The federal reasonable efforts requirement is not relevant in a TPR proceeding, where the issue is whether to terminate a temporary foster care placement and family reunification efforts.[12]

At the TPR proceeding stage of a case, the court is to address the appropriateness of terminating the child's temporary foster care placement in light of the inability of the parents to provide an adequate home for the child within a reasonable time, and in light of the child's need for a timely permanent placement. At this stage, the agency's culpability in previously failing to make reasonable efforts to provide services to the parents is irrelevant. The only point on which agency services would be relevant is in determining whether the parents could provide an adequate home within a reasonable time to meet the child's needs for timely permanence. This point, however, would involve proof concerning possible future services to the parents, not a rehashing of the alleged inadequacies of past services. If the agency's failures concerning past services are deemed relevant in a TPR proceeding, there will be a high risk of punishing children for the agency's failures by keeping them in temporary foster care placements and denying them the timely permanence they need to develop properly.[13]

The Michigan statutory grounds that allow for TPR do not include a requirement that the agency prove it has made reasonable efforts to reunite the family. Once the TPR stage has been reached, under the Michigan statutory scheme, the cases fall into two categories.

In the first category are cases where the parents' ability to provide an adequate home in the foreseeable future is basically nonexistent (i.e., cases involving desertion or serious physical abuse that will continue despite services). In these cases, providing services would be futile, and the agency's failure to provide adequate services is completely irrelevant. The second category consists of cases where the child has been removed from the parental home for a period in excess of six months and the parent has made no progress in rectifying the conditions that led to removal. In these long-term neglect cases, the focus should be on the child's need for immediate permanence, and not on the agency's failure to provide services to the parents. Imposing a reasonable-efforts requirement at this point in the case would only further harm the child by allowing the agency's failures to preclude a TPR order.

It is reasonable to require an agency to make reasonable efforts before obtaining federal funds for ongoing family foster care placements, but this is all that federal law is designed to require. Once family foster care no longer serves the child's best interests and the child needs a timely permanent placement, the court's only focus should be the statutory grounds for TPR and whether TPR is in the child's best interests. The agency's conduct should be irrelevant, and the statutory grounds for TPR should not work to deny the child's need for permanence by including a reasonable-efforts requirement that brings the agency's conduct into the proceeding.

An agency attorney who practices in a jurisdiction where the conduct of the agency is considered relevant in TPR proceedings should consider working toward legislative reform to remove this impediment to permanence for children. The agency will still have a substantial incentive to make reasonable efforts in order to obtain federal funding for family foster care placements. This federal funding requirement is adequate incentive, if properly enforced, and should not be extended to become a part of the state's statutory grounds for TPR. There it will only hinder the agency's efforts to obtain timely permanent placements for children.

Products of the Agency Attorney Project

A detailed analysis of project case data has yielded two main products.

Data Analysis

First, the project has generated data that permit a comparison of the private and public models of legal representation. The bottom-line measure in the comparison is the effectiveness of each model in achieving a timely agency permanency decision for a child. The data analysis also includes a comparison of many other factors, such as the level of attorney services and social worker satisfaction under each model.

The private model project attorney had, as of March 1, 1991, achieved a timely agency permanency decision that could be quickly achieved in Michigan courts in 100% of her cases. The vast majority (over 96%) of these agency permanency decisions were achieved within one year of the date when the initial dispositional hearings in project cases were completed. The social worker clients in project cases have consistently and enthusiastically expressed their satisfaction with the project attorney in comparison to assistant prosecutors.

The data analysis also includes a cost-benefit comparison of the two models of legal representation that justifies the economic benefits to state agencies of contracting with attorneys under the private model. The project attorney achieved permanency decisions for children substantially earlier than the local prosecutors. For example, for cases that proceeded to a TPR hearing in one county (approximately 12% of that county's total cases), TPR was achieved, on average, more than 250 days earlier in cases handled by the project attorney. Thus, the private model leads to a significant saving in foster care expenditures. This cost saving, when combined with the cost saving from the salaries of the local prosecutors (computed as a portion of the assistant prosecuting attorney's salary related to child abuse and neglect litigation, since agencies do not pay directly for the local prosecutor's services), outweighs the increased cost to the agency of contracting with attorneys who provide legal services under the private model approach.

In order to make cost comparisons between the two models, the project attorney maintained detailed records of the time she spent on each case. The cost to the agency of employing private-model attorneys was computed at a reasonable market hourly rate. This private-model cost was then compared with the cost for legal services under the public model and the higher costs for foster care incurred under the public model. Of course, even if the private model, when actually implemented, costs slightly more in dollars, the benefits to children of timely agency permanency decisions will certainly justify the incremental cost.

It should be noted that current Michigan law allows DSS to engage private counsel if the local prosecutor "does not" appear. When contacted at the beginning of this project, prosecutors initially hesitated to give up control over child abuse and neglect cases. They yielded to private counsel for DSS, however, once they were assured that they would continue to prosecute any crimes involving child abuse and neglect offenses. In Michigan, therefore, DSS could engage private counsel in a competitive bid system that would ensure a high degree of attorney motivation to serve the client (DSS) and would free the agency attorney from political considerations concerning career advancement within a governmental unit separate from the agency. Agencies in other states may already be free to engage private counsel, or may sponsor legislation to allow such procedures if the results of this project are seen to justify such reform.

Agency Attorney Training Manual

The second major product of the project is a training manual for attorneys representing the state agency in child abuse and neglect matters under the private model of legal representation. The material in the training manual is based on the real case experiences of the project attorney and observations of the work of local prosecutors. The case experiences of the project attorney also include feedback from social worker clients concerning their satisfaction with both models of legal representation.

This manual provides detailed, pragmatic guidance to agency attorneys implementing the private model of legal representation in civil child protection proceedings. The manual first outlines, in detail, the Michigan law applicable in civil child protection proceedings in the four project counties, then discusses interdisciplinary training for attorneys and the methods used for determining and assessing services provided dysfunctional families in a particular community. It describes the initial social worker contact and the petition writing process. Finally, the manual sets out, in detail, the private model approach at each stage of a child protection proceeding—preliminary hearing, pretrial conference, trial, initial dispositional hearing, periodic dispositional review hearings, permanency hearing, and the termination of parental rights hearing. The discussion of each stage includes specifics about meetings and interactions with the social workers.

Implementation of the approach to legal representation set out in the manual should substantially improve the ability of state agencies and juvenile courts to serve the best interests of children by timely application of permanency planning concepts.

Notes

1. Maluccio, A.N.; Fein, E.; and Olmstead, K. *Permanency Planning for Children,* New York: Tavistock Publications, 1986: 5–6.
2. Maluccio et al., 26–28.
3. P.L. 96-272, *42 USC* § 670 et seq.
4. Maluccio et al., 36.
5. Maluccio et al., 49.
6. American Bar Association, *Foster Children in the Courts,* National Legal Resource Center for Child Advocacy and Protection, Austin, TX: Butterworth Legal Publishers, 1983: 45–49.
7. American Bar Association (ABA), *American Bar Association Model Rules for Professional Conduct,* Chicago: ABA, 1981: 1.2, 1.4, and 1.13.
8. For a general description of the private model, see Horowitz, "Child Protection Agencies," *Vermont Law Review* 6, 381 (1981): 394–401.
9. Michigan Compiled Laws (MCL) 712A.
10. Michigan Court Rules (MCR) 5.965 to 974. All specific references to Michigan law that follow may be found in either MCL or MCR in the sections cited.

11. See M. Garrison, "Child Welfare Decisionmaking: In Search of the Least Drastic Alternative," *Georgetown Law Journal* 75, (1987): 1745, note 160, citing E. Weinstein, *The Self Image of the Foster Child*: 66–67 (significant relationship between number of placements and emotional development); Caplan and Douglas, "Incidence of Parental Loss in Children with Depressed Moods," *Journal of Child Psychology and Psychiatry* 10 (1969): 225, 227 (significantly higher incidence of depression in children subject to more than one foster placement).
12. *In re. D.G.*, 583 A.2d 160 (D.C. App. 1990).
13. *In the Matter of Sheila G.*, 61 N.Y. 2d 368, 474 N.Y.S. 2d 421, 462 N.E. 2d 1139 (1984).

Reference List: Interdisciplinary Readings

Causes and Incidence of Child Abuse and Neglect

Besharov, D. "The Child Abuse Numbers Game." *Wall Street Journal*, August 4, 1988.

Daro, D., and McCurdy, K. *Current Trends in Child Abuse Reporting and Fatalities: The Results of the 1991 Annual Fifty-State Survey.* Chicago: The National Committee for Prevention of Child Abuse, 1992.

Faller, K. *Child Sexual Abuse: An Interdisciplinary Manual for Diagnosis, Case Management, and Treatment.* New York: Columbia University Press, 1988.

Faller, K., and Ziefert, M. "Causes of Child Abuse and Neglect." In *Social Work with Abused and Neglected Children: A Manual of Interdisciplinary Practice*, edited by K. Faller. New York: The Free Press, 1981.

Magrab, P. *Psychological and Behavioral Assessment: Impact on Pediatric Care.* New York: Plenum Publishing, 1984, 337–345.

Basic Child Development

Fraiberg, S. *Clinical Studies in Infant Mental Health: The First Year of Life.* New York: Basic Books, 1980.

Kleinman, J. "Functional Tasks of Child Development." In *Social Work with Abused and Neglected Children: A Manual of Interdisciplinary Practice*, edited by K. Faller. New York: The Free Press, 1981.

Robertson, James, and Robertson, Joyce. "Young Children in Brief Separation: A Fresh Look." In *Psychoanalytic Study of the Child*, Vol. 26, edited by Ruth S. Eissler. New Haven: Yale University Press, 1971.

Thompson, A.E. "Normal Child Development." In *Social Work with Abused and Neglected Children: A Manual of Interdisciplinary Practice*, edited by K. Faller. New York: The Free Press, 1981.

Thompson A.E. "Making the Decision to Separate Child and Family." In *Social Work with Abused and Neglected Children: A Manual of Interdisciplinary Practice*, edited by K. Faller. New York: The Free Press, 1981.

Specific Medical Problems Indicating Child Abuse and Neglect

Meadow, R. "Munchausen Syndrome by Proxy: The Hinterland of Child Abuse." *The Lancet,* August 13, 1977.

Oates, R.K., and Hufton, I.W. "The Spectrum of Failure to Thrive and Child Abuse: A Follow Up Study." In *Child Abuse and Neglect* 1 (1977): 119–124.

Assessing and Treating the Family

Jones, D.P.H. "The Untreatable Family." In *Child Abuse and Neglect* 11, 3 (1987): 409–420.

Steinhauer, P. "Assessing for Parenting Capacity." *American Journal of Orthopsychiatry* 53, 3 (July 1983): 468–481.

Sexual Abuse

Jaudes, P.K., and Morris, M. "Child Sexual Abuse: Who Goes Home?" *Child Abuse and Neglect* 14, 1 (1990), 61–68.

Sgroi, S. *Handbook of Clinical Interventions in Child Sexual Abuse.* Lexington, MA: Lexington Books, 1982.

Standards for State Intervention

Wald, M. "State Intervention on Behalf Of 'Neglected' Children: A Search For Realistic Standards." *Stanford Law Review* 27, 4 (1975): 985–1040

Goldstein, J.; Freud, A.; and Solnit, A. *Before the Best Interests of the Child.* New York: The Free Press, 1979.

Permanency Planning

Maluccio, A.N.; Fein, E.; and Olmstead, K. *Permanency Planning for Children.* New York: Tavistock Publications, 1986.

CHAPTER 3

Changing Agency Procedures

Debra Ratterman

Drawn-out court hearings, excessive adjournments, suspended decisions, and long appeals characterize the process of freeing children in foster care for adoption. Most of the delays, however, happen long before a petition is filed. Examining agency procedures for permanency planning is a good place to start in tackling impediments to termination of parental rights (TPR).

The New York State Termination Barriers Project, conducted by the American Bar Association (ABA) Center on Children and the Law, found that children were kept in foster care for years before the agency considered freeing them for adoption. Poor communication and coordination between caseworkers and attorneys slowed efforts to begin TPR actions. Agency staff members did not know enough about the law on termination of parental rights to feel confident in their decisions to file petitions. Finally, layoffs and high staff turnover hurt efforts to achieve permanence for children in care.

The project was conducted in two New York counties, Onondaga County and Chemung County. Onondaga is a large urban county with a population of approximately 500,000 people, 200,000 of them in the city of Syracuse. The county had 850 children in care in 1988—a very high number compared to similar counties in New York. Only 60 of these children, 7% of the family foster care population, had been officially identified for TPR and adoption, and only 17 TPR petitions were pending. In contrast,

Chemung County is a small county with a mixed urban and rural population. Approximately 100,000 people live in the county; the largest city, Elmira, has a population of 30,000. The county department of social services had 182 children in foster care in 1988. No TPR petitions were filed in that year.

The two-year, $200,000 ABA project reduced the amount of time children spent in care in the two project counties by more than a year, achieving permanence for children and saving over $2 million in foster care costs.

Identifying Children for Adoption

Throughout the country, many children remain in out-of-home care for several years before a decision is made to seek termination of parental rights. In one of the project counties, children spent an average of 3.5 years in care before a referral was made to begin a TPR action. If the case involved sexual abuse or a mentally ill parent, the average delay was five years.

State statutes usually set the period of time a child must be in care before a TPR action can be brought. The time period may be different for each ground, or basis for action. In New York state, a child must be in care for one year before an action can be filed on the ground of permanent neglect. For abandoned children, the time period is six months. It is rare, however, for any TPR ground to require that a child be in foster care for more than a year.

Permanency planning specialists recommend that a permanent placement decision be made after a child has been in care for 12 to 18 months. Except in special cases, children should be returned home or freed for adoption at this point. The chances of children ever returning to their biological parents fall dramatically after one year in out-of-home care.

Although there are usually no statutory barriers to early identification of children for whom adoption is the appropriate goal, institutional obstacles may prevent these decisions from being made promptly. To remove these obstacles, the project inaugurated three policy improvements: permanency planning specialists, a TPR checklist, and permanency planning committees.

Permanency Planning Specialists

One reason caseworkers are often reluctant to recommend TPR is that they have built a working relationship with the family in their efforts to achieve reunification. They often find it difficult to step back and reconsider whether further efforts will be successful or whether adoption might be better for the child. Having a full-time staff member with casework experience to review these cases and consider adoption among other options can help caseworkers make the difficult decision to proceed with a TPR action. This permanency planning specialist can also help caseworkers prepare a case for the attorney and act as a liaison between the casework staff and whoever does the legal work on TPR cases.

The permanency planning specialist can build up expertise in the practical and legal aspects of TPR that will benefit the entire staff, and can informally train staff members on TPR law and procedures. Most important, the specialist can give caseworkers the support they need to get through the long and difficult process of terminating parental rights.

The TPR Checklist

Another problem that inhibits caseworkers from recommending that a foster child be freed for adoption is uncertainty about TPR law. For example, some New York caseworkers were not aware of changes in the state's laws that allowed TPR actions to be filed against incarcerated parents. State law on termination of parental rights is written in dense legal language. Courts may vary in their interpretation of the law. Caseworkers needed a clear and concise way to see how fact and law fit together.

This project summarized the legal requirements in a checklist format so that caseworkers can find out quickly whether they can free a child for adoption. The TPR checklist (reproduced at the end of this chapter) makes sure that caseworkers consider each potential ground for TPR as well as the special aspects of each case that might excuse certain elements or require additional proof.

The checklist should cover the legal elements for each ground, the rights to participation or notice of putative fathers, special requirements for Native American children, and the child's prospects for adoption. It should be designed to be completed in 15 to 20 minutes. Most of the questions should require only a yes or no checkoff. On the checklist the project developed, only one question—on the original reason for placement—asks for a short narrative answer. This format enables the caseworker to view the checklist as a decision-making tool, not another required form that must be laboriously filled out. Experienced caseworkers can use portions of the checklist as needed. The project recommended that the checklist be used at the time a child has been in care for one year (or six months if there has been no contact with a parent), but each agency can develop a TPR checklist to fit its own state laws.

The Permanency Planning Committee

The permanency planning committee is another useful tool for making sure that children do not remain unnecessarily long in temporary family foster care placements. All states have some type of case review at least every 18 months, but a separate permanency planning committee review at the one-year mark focuses discussion on the possibility of termination of parental rights. The key difference between the permanency planning committee and existing case review bodies is the participation of an attorney to assess the legal aspects of the case.

The first step in setting up a permanency planning committee in an agency is to develop written goals and procedures. In the project counties, a one-page protocol outlined when cases would be reviewed, who would participate, and how the meeting would be run. This protocol was then presented to the staff as one part of a training program conducted by the project.

Two models for permanency planning committees were developed, based on the differing needs of the project counties. The Onondaga County model is an internal review in which agency staff members discuss cases strategically. The Chemung County model includes parents, service providers, foster parents, and the children's attorney, who join the staff in a full-scale review of the case.

In Onondaga County

The permanency planning review panel comprises the director of the children's division; supervisors from the child protection, family foster care, and preventive services units; a representative of the county attorney's office; and the permanency planning specialist, who serves as facilitator. The panel reviews a case when the child has been in placement for 16 months. This period was chosen because a large number of children in Onondaga County are returned to their families after 13 to 15 months in placement.

The caseworker goes over the TPR checklist before the meeting. At the meeting, the caseworker presents the family's service history, any impediments to reunification, and an assessment of the potential for termination of parental rights. The review of each case is limited to 15 to 30 minutes. The permanency planning specialist schedules the reviews, notifies the caseworkers assigned to cases chosen for review, and keeps the minutes for the panel.

At the end of the discussion, a plan of action is agreed on. If the decision is to file for TPR, the permanency planning specialist will set a time to help the caseworker get started. If TPR is not yet appropriate, or the panel wants more information or wants the caseworker to try a new approach, the case is reset for review at a later date.

Caseworkers in Onondaga County have found the permanency planning review panel a useful forum for discussing difficult cases. Some caseworkers have even requested that their older cases be reviewed by the panel. The number of terminations of parental rights filed in the county more than tripled in the year following implementation of the panel.

In Chemung County

The permanency planning committee reviews cases when a child has been in care for one year, to coincide with the court's required 12–month service plan review for extension of placement. Both reviews take place on the same day.

Committee meetings are held in two parts. In the first part, the supervisor, the caseworker, the agency attorney, any other appropriate agency representative, the law guardian, a court-appointed special advocate (CASA) if assigned, foster parents, biological parents, and the permanency planning chair conduct the service plan review. In the second part, the same participants discuss whether a TPR action should be filed.

In preparation for this review, the caseworker is asked to complete the checklist. The permanency planning specialist sets up the reviews, keeps the minutes, and monitors cases for which TPR is recommended.

Chemung County staff members have been pleased with their permanency planning committee. In many cases, the first committee meeting was the first time all the service providers had been together in one room to discuss a family's progress. The parents' attendance has been crucial. Several parents have agreed to surrender a child after participating in the meeting. One child was returned to her mother after all the service providers agreed that the mother had made significant progress.

Case Preparation

Preparing a case before filing the TPR petition has been another source of delay. Caseworkers and attorneys are often reluctant to begin this process because TPR cases take a long time to organize and prepare. Because other court actions, like temporary removals or fact-finding hearings, have strict time deadlines, TPR cases are often given low priority. Caseworkers and attorneys may also be unclear about their respective responsibilities in case preparation. Confusion and miscommunication result.

To remedy this problem, a written protocol was developed outlining the respective duties of caseworkers and attorneys in starting a TPR action. New forms helped organize case information for the TPR petition, for evidence on efforts to reunify the family, and for affidavits for substituted service (such as publication of a notice in the newspaper) in cases involving missing parents. New procedures improved attorney-caseworker communication on TPR cases.

The Caseworker-Attorney Protocol

In addition to dividing responsibilities for case preparation, the protocol sets time limits for each step to make sure the petition is filed promptly after the decision to free a child for adoption is made. A model protocol developed by the ABA Center on Children and the Law was modified to fit the needs of each county. In Onondaga County, the case reviews showed that it had taken an average of six months from the time a case was referred to the legal department to the filing of the petition. Under the then-existing procedure for TPR cases, the caseworker made a written referral to the legal department to set up a TPR conference. Before that conference, the caseworker was asked to complete a form with factual information on the case.

The new procedure consolidated the referral process into one form, the TPR checklist. This form must be completed within 30 days of the decision to terminate parental rights, and a meeting with the attorney must be held within 15 days of the completion of the checklist. The petition must be filed within 30 days after this meeting. As a result of this new protocol, the length of time between referral and petition has been cut in half.

In Chemung County, a shortage of legal staff requires that the caseworkers perform a substantial portion of the case preparation, including drafting the petition and the accompanying affidavit. Under their attorney-caseworker protocol, the caseworkers must complete these tasks within 45 days after the decision to seek TPR is made, or within 60 days if a search must be made for a missing parent. The attorney must meet with the caseworker to review these materials within one week of their completion. Within 10 days of this meeting, the attorney must file the petition. Protocols can vary with staffing patterns. If an agency has paralegal staff members, they may be assigned to write petitions, file subpoenas, and draft affidavits. If one caseworker has been assigned to specialize in legal work, he or she can work with the child's caseworker to draft the petition and prepare the case for trial.

Using the TPR Checklist

The checklist developed to help the caseworker determine whether a TPR action is legally viable in any particular case is also an excellent tool for organizing a case before preparation of the petition. The checklist should ask for the names and addresses of the parties who must receive notice of the action. It should also provide a checkoff of necessary documentation for filing the petition, such as the child's birth certificate. The checklist of legal requirements enables the attorney to readily identify any legal elements that are likely to be contested in the case. A section summarizing previous medical and psychological evaluations could be added when expert testimony in those areas is appropriate.

The Agency Efforts Outline

Many, but not all, grounds for termination of parental rights require the agency to show that it has made efforts to reunify the family. In New York, the agency must show that it has made "diligent efforts" to encourage and strengthen the parental relationship in permanent neglect TPRs. Because reunification efforts must necessarily be determined on a case-by-case basis, taking into consideration the special circumstances of each case, agency staff members are often unsure when their efforts have been sufficiently diligent to allow them to bring a TPR action successfully.

Despite the inherent flexibility of the diligent efforts standard, New York law does provide some specific guidelines for determining whether the standard has been met. For example, the statute defines *diligent efforts* to include consulting with the family in developing the service plan, making arrangements for visiting, providing needed support services and assistance, and informing the parents of the child's progress and well-being. In other states, the courts have offered still more specific guidance as to what reunification efforts the agency should undertake.

To aid caseworkers and attorneys in preparing and organizing evidence on agency efforts, the project developed an outline based on the New York statutory definition and incorporating the insights of case law on this issue. This diligent efforts outline provides both a checklist to evaluate whether efforts have been sufficient and a framework for persuasive organization of evidence on the agency's efforts.

The law in any state can be used to develop a similar outline. It should include the family's service plan, a summary of the parents' visits, and a list of services offered the family. In some cases, the parent is so dangerous or the problems so intractable that reunification efforts would be detrimental to the best interests of the child. The outline should provide a section to explain suspension of the parents' visits or termination of services in such cases.

Like many states, New York requires for certain TPR grounds that the agency show it made diligent efforts to strengthen and rehabilitate the family. Because this determination must be made on a case-by-case basis, there is a great deal of uncertainty about how best to present this information to the court.

The Chemung County Department of Social Services routinely attaches an affidavit to each TPR petition that recounts all the efforts made by the agency to reunite the family. Before this project, the affidavits were done in chronological order, and, given the complexity of most cases, were difficult to follow. Many were 50 or more pages long and took the caseworker weeks to prepare. A specific format for this affidavit was clearly needed to help caseworkers focus on the most important factual information and to ensure that all the statutory elements of diligent efforts were met.

Using the diligent efforts outline the project developed, a case-worker is now able to make a persuasive case for TPR, and the attorney for the agency is able to prepare and present comprehensive testimony on efforts to reunify the family. The affidavits are concise, easy to read, and quick to complete.

Onondaga County also needed guidance in preparing evidence and testimony on diligent efforts. The diligent efforts outline caseworkers had used to determine if the requirement was being met was shortened to meet Onondaga County's needs. This new format helps a caseworker to determine if the diligent efforts requirement may be waived under the special circumstances of a particular case. It also outlines the special conditions that obtain when parents are incarcerated.

The Missing Parents Checklist

Before filing a legal action, the agency must try to locate both parents so they can be served with the petition. Ideally, the agency should maintain contact with the parents and initiate a search as soon as they appear to be missing. If a parent cannot be found, the agency must document to the court that it has made a diligent search. If the judge is satisfied with the agency's efforts to find the parent, he or she can order substituted service, such as publication of a notice in the newspaper. Many agencies experience delays in filing TPR actions because caseworkers are unsure of how to make a search. In the project counties, 25 to 50% of the TPR cases involved at least one missing parent, so a checklist was developed to clarify and standardize the procedure for these cases.

The missing parents checklist records actions such as letters sent to the last known address, contacts with relatives and neighbors, and checks with governmental agencies. In large agencies, it may be desirable to assign a full-time member of the office staff to conduct these searches. Other agencies might coordinate searches with their child support divisions. If caseworkers must search for missing parents, they should be given a checklist.

Caseworker-Attorney Communication

A lack of communication between agency attorneys and caseworkers is the major problem that delays the preparation of TPR cases. Many caseworkers express frustration at being unable to talk to an attorney when they have a legal question, need information on the status of a case, or want clarification of a request from the attorney. Attorneys are also frustrated, because of the inadequate time they are given to prepare and what they consider to be inadequate documentation and preparation by the caseworkers.

Many of the reforms discussed above will indirectly ameliorate these problems. Protocols help to clarify what is expected of caseworkers and attorneys. Checklists and forms standardize the information the caseworker provides to the attorney. The time limits placed on specific tasks give both caseworkers and attorneys realistic expectations for when work will be completed.

The project also tackled the problem of attorney-caseworker communication. We found Segal [1988] an important resource for coping with this problem. Because of the differences among agencies in the size and organization of legal staff, changes should be tailored to each agency.

In one project county, communication was enhanced by the assignment of one attorney to handle all TPR referrals. This attorney participates in the permanency planning review panel and is present at all TPR conferences to identify any legal obstacles to freeing a child for adoption. The attorney also drafts and files the TPR petition. In addition, this attorney holds biweekly question-and-answer sessions for all children's division staff members at which she responds to written questions submitted before the meeting.

Legal Analysis

The lack of knowledge of state law on specific legal issues is another problem that causes delays in termination of parental rights actions. As part of this project, the ABA consultant researched and compiled current statutory and case law on several issues: the diligent efforts requirement, exceptions to the diligent efforts requirement, putative fathers, mental illness/retardation terminations, surrenders, and the Indian Child Welfare Act.

TPR law varies considerably from state to state. Each agency should focus on the critical legal issues in its state. The agency can do its own legal analysis or hire consultants to analyze the law. The following summary indicates what the project found in researching New York law.

Diligent Efforts

Grounds for termination of parental rights in New York, as in many other states, require the agency to prove that it has made diligent efforts to encourage and strengthen the parental relationship. Uncertainty as to whether the agency has met this elusive standard makes caseworkers reluctant to recommend TPR, and attorneys reluctant to bring TPR actions. Since the definition of *diligent efforts* has been litigated extensively in New York courts, participants in the TPR process would clearly benefit from an analysis of the case law.

The best summary of New York law on the diligent efforts requirements is Spinak [1989]. According to Spinak's analysis, diligent efforts is the first issue the court must resolve in determining whether the grounds for permanent neglect have been met. Courts have stressed the importance of the service plan for reunification of the family. Although each court's findings on diligent efforts are fact-specific, and family court judges have a significant degree of discretion in this matter, the majority of courts will find that diligent efforts have been made if the agency has made reasonable attempts to assist the family.

Spinak analyzed appellate cases on diligent efforts since the landmark Court of Appeals case, the 1984 *Sheila G.*, and found that appellate courts were likely to uphold lower court findings that diligent efforts had been made, and also likely to reverse lower court findings that diligent efforts had not been made. She concludes that the diligent efforts requirement is not the insurmountable obstacle to termination of parental rights that it is sometimes perceived to be.

Exceptions to Diligent Efforts

After reviewing the legal analysis of diligent efforts, the project did follow-up research on special circumstances in which exceptions to the diligent efforts requirement could be made. Some TPR actions were not brought because efforts had not been made to reunite the family. In addition, there was confusion as to whether a TPR could be brought if a parent's visiting has been suspended to protect the child.

In New York, there are three legally recognized exceptions to the diligent efforts requirement that can be used to pursue TPR in some cases: when parents have failed to keep the agency apprised of their address for at least six months, when an incarcerated parent has failed to cooperate with the agency on more than one occasion, and when efforts to reunite the family would be detrimental to the child.

An agency's suspension of parental visiting does not prevent the agency from seeking termination of the parents' rights. TPR cannot be sought on the grounds of abandonment, in this case, or for failure to contact the child, when permanent neglect is the ground. However, parents can be alleged to have permanently neglected the child by failing to plan for a child's future if they have failed to resolve the problems that led to the suspension of visiting.

Putative Fathers

Another source of delay in TPR actions is confusion over the right of an unwed father to block an adoption or offer evidence on whether a TPR should be granted. The project provided a summary of New York law on this question to clarify when fathers must be included in or notified of TPR actions and as a step toward establishing uniform procedures and policies in this regard. New York law sets forth clear standards for determining the rights of unmarried fathers when a child's adoption is at issue. It establishes a three-tier system: (1) fathers whose rights must be surrendered or terminated before the child can be adopted ("consent fathers"), (2) fathers who are entitled to notice of an action to terminate the mother's rights so they can present evidence on the child's best interests ("notice fathers"), and (3) fathers who have no right to block an adoption or present evidence. The courts have strictly construed the statutory requirements for consent. In cases where a father's consent is clearly not required for adoption, the TPR action should not be delayed by attempts to include the putative father or notify him of the action.

Parents with Mental Illness or Retardation

In its case reviews, the project found that children with mentally ill parents or parents with developmental disabilities often lingered for long periods in family foster care. The New York law on TPR on the basis of mental illness or retardation was analyzed to assess why these cases were slow to move toward resolution.

Under New York law, parental rights can be terminated if, by reason of mental illness or mental retardation, parents are presently and for the foreseeable future unable to provide proper and adequate care for their children. The law requires the court to appoint an expert to evaluate the parent. Parents are entitled to have their attorney present during this evaluation. The tough question in these TPR cases is whether the parent will remain unable to care for the child "in the foreseeable future." Experts are often reluctant to make such pessimistic assessments. There is a trend in the case law, however, to place some weight on parents' failure to progress in the past. As a result, parents' medical history and their lack of cooperation in services are becoming an important part of the agency's case.

Surrenders

New York surrender law has recently gone through several transformations. These changes in forms and procedures have left caseworkers uncertain about how to proceed when parents wish to give up their parental rights voluntarily.

The current law sets up a special procedure for parents who surrender children already in foster care. The new surrender instrument clearly states that the parent is giving up all rights to custody and to visit with, speak with, write to, or learn about the child forever. It does, however, give parents the option of joining the adoption information register, which allows adopted children to get information about their biological parents after they turn 18.

The agency has the choice of obtaining a judicial or an extrajudicial surrender. A judicial surrender must be signed before a family court judge, who must inform parents of their right to an attorney and to supportive counseling. Parents must also be asked whether they understand the consequences of the surrender and whether the agency agreed to any special terms. Open adoption is allowed, under the statute, but all terms must be written into the surrender. A judicial surrender is final and irrevocable once it is signed, so an adoption proceeding can begin immediately.

An extrajudicial surrender is signed outside of court before two witnesses. The law requires that one of the witnesses be a trained agency employee and the other a certified social worker or attorney unaffiliated with the agency. The agency must apply for judicial approval of the surrender within 15 days of its signing. An extrajudicial surrender can be revoked by the parent for any reason within 45 days. It is also revocable after 45 days if the child is not in an adoptive placement.

Because of the complex procedures for extrajudicial surrenders, the difficulty of finding a nonemployee witness, and the long period of revocability, the project recommended that New York agencies use the judicial surrender only.

The Indian Child Welfare Act

Freeing a Native American child for adoption requires that caseworkers understand the Indian Child Welfare Act of 1978 (ICWA). The act applies to all children who are members of Indian tribes and all children of tribal members who are eligible for membership. Congress passed the Indian Child Welfare Act to rectify the misuse of state child protective authority in removing Indian children and placing them with non-Indian families. Before the passage of the ICWA, Indian children were placed in foster care or for adoption in New York State at three times the rate of non-Indian children. The ICWA seeks to ensure that Indian tribes will be able to intervene so that culturally sensitive decisions can be made.

The Indian Child Welfare Act sets certain requirements for out-of-home placement and TPR decisions involving Native American children. The major provisions require:

- notice to tribes and Indian custodians;
- transfers to tribal courts in some cases;
- recognition of the tribal right to intervene in state court cases;
- proof of emotional or physical harm to the child before she or he is removed from the parents or parental rights are terminated;
- "active efforts" to prevent removal and to reunify Indian families;
- informed consent to voluntary placements and surrenders, along with special rights to revoke these instruments; and
- placement preferences for extended family members and Native American families.

Although the ICWA places special requirements on cases involving Native American children, it does not prevent the court from freeing these children for adoption. As long as the mandates of the act are followed, Native American children in foster care can be given permanent homes.

Technical Assistance

Agencies can deal competently with local issues that create delays if they have access to good technical assistance. At the request of the project counties, the ABA Center on Children and the Law has provided technical assistance on problems relating to termination of parental rights in the form of full-day case consultations, special advice on difficult cases, and liaison work with the family court. Having technical assistance on TPR readily available saves time for both attorneys and caseworkers in preparing and presenting TPR cases.

Training

Legal training for all agency staff is a key component of the reform package the project developed. A comprehensive understanding of the legal prerequisites for termination of parental rights and expanded skills in case preparation and presentation reduce delay in several ways. The reluctance of caseworkers and attorneys to bring TPR actions diminishes as the standards for success in these actions become clearer. Caseworkers and attorneys are able to prepare winning cases. Finally, less time is wasted in litigating issues clearly resolved by existing law.

Training Needs Assessment

The project conducted an assessment to determine in what legal areas caseworkers, supervisors, and attorneys felt the need for training. Two programs developed caseworkers' expertise. The first covered the basics in child welfare law to give new caseworkers more understanding and confidence in court proceedings; the second focused on the legal requirements for termination of parental rights.

To avoid any overlap with training already offered in the region, the needs assessment instrument listed specific legal issues and asked respondents to rate their need for training in each on a scale of 1 to 10. The instrument also asked what legal skill training was needed, who should be included in the training, what training methods were preferred, and what were the best days for training to be held.

This survey revealed significant gaps in legal training on termination of parental rights, particularly for caseworkers. In Onondaga County, those surveyed wanted training on all aspects of TPR, but especially on permanent neglect and the diligent efforts requirement, procedures for surrenders, and how to use earlier court proceedings to enforce the goals of the service plan. In Chemung County, a significant number of respondents wanted training on reducing delays in TPR cases, caseworker testimony, and the use of expert witnesses. It was surprising to find considerable need for training on virtually all the issues listed in the survey.

Child Welfare Law Training

The first training, "Introduction to Child Welfare Law," was conducted by mail—a relatively inexpensive option—in order to test its usefulness for certain training needs. Specially prepared training materials were sent to the caseworkers of the Chemung County Department of Social Services and the attorneys of the Onondaga County Department of Social Services.

These materials offered a general introduction to child welfare law; a step-by-step guide to voluntary placements, child abuse and neglect proceedings, and TPR/surrenders; and a review of recent statutory changes. Two weeks after the materials were sent, three days were allotted for the ABA consultant to answer questions phoned in on these materials.

This type of training bypassed the need to schedule around the particularly strenuous schedules of staff members and allowed trainees at different experience levels to review the materials at their own pace, while still giving trainees access to the trainer for their individual questions and problems. This plan was relatively successful in conveying the necessary information. The same material was used in onsite training for Onondaga County caseworkers.

Termination of Parental Rights Training

The ABA consultant presented direct training on termination of parental rights law to the attorneys and caseworkers of both counties. The trainees were given copies of all the forms and protocols developed by the project, and each was explained in detail. Trainees were also given a legal summary of TPR law, along with the special legal case analyses developed for the project. The TPR checklist was used as an outline for a discussion of legal issues in these cases.

In Onondaga County, a trainer from the state department of social services also presented a particularly innovative session, "How to Survive TPR," on the emotional difficulties that caseworkers face in this type of litigation.

Implementing Agency Reform

Change always creates anxiety. At every stage in efforts to reduce delay, it is important to keep everyone involved in the TPR process aware of what is taking place.

Within the Agency

To inform the staff about the project's plan to reduce delays in freeing children for adoption and to allay fears, brief presentations were made to the staff members of both county departments at the beginning of the project. Their response was positive, because many had been frustrated in their efforts to free children for adoption. Hearing the staff's comments, concerns, and hopes at the beginning of the project put planning on a solid foundation and increased opportunities to introduce reforms successfully.

The permanency planning specialists were able to disseminate information about the project both formally and informally. One specialist developed a children's division newsletter. The specialists enhanced the project's ability to observe and understand local TPR practice, to respond quickly to pressing needs, and to incorporate ongoing feedback from staff members about the changes being implemented.

In retrospect, it probably would have been better for the project if the ABA consultant had spent more time onsite. The consultant spent a week in each county for case reviews and made bimonthly trips to attend advisory board and other project meetings and to conduct training. She was also available by phone to answer questions or to consult on particular cases. More time onsite would have given the consultant greater opportunities to interact with the staff—some of the best suggestions came from the casework staff and the attorneys—and to provide more immediate technical support as reforms were implemented.

With Outside Systems

An advisory board was created to make sure that all the key participants in the TPR process would be involved in efforts to reduce delays. Each county brought together representatives from the state and local departments of social services and the family court, as well as the county attorney, law guardians, parents' attorneys, foster parents, child advocacy groups, CASA representatives, and other interested parties, to form the advisory boards. The advisory boards met every two months to review progress, to develop and comment on reform proposals, and to evaluate and modify changes that had been instituted. All the advisory board members have made important contributions to the project's work. Each advisory board also functions as a medium to circulate information about the project to those directly involved in TPR litigation. In New York, it was especially important to involve advocacy groups like the Task Force on Permanency Planning for Foster Children, the Law Guardian Back-Up Center, and the New York State Citizens' Coalition for Children, to make information about the project available beyond the two project counties.

To make the legal analyses developed by the project available to legal practitioners around the state and the country, articles were submitted to legal journals. An initial press release and articles in the local media and in child advocacy publications were important in informing the public about the project.

An interim report and a final report disseminated comprehensive information about the ongoing work. The reports summarized the project, described its findings, discussed how innovations reduced delays, and offered guidance in reproducing the project's efforts to other counties and states. The reports were distributed to the children's services director of each New York county department of social services, to New York family court judges, and to selected child advocacy groups, as well as to others interested in avoiding delays in freeing children for adoption.

The Problem of Inadequate Resources

Delays in freeing children for adoption cannot be reduced solely by improving the efficiency of the child welfare agency. No system will be able to assure children the permanent, safe, and stable homes they need until child protective agencies are provided with sufficient resources to fulfill their statutory duties.

The financial and emotional costs of foster care drift far outweigh the cost of the additional resources that allow a child welfare system to work expeditiously toward permanency for children. In passing legislation to provide housing subsidies for families of children in out-of-home care, the New York State Legislature noted that maintaining a child in family foster care for one year cost, on the average, $10,000 to $15,000. Add to this the psychological cost for children who spend years of their childhood in temporary placements. Increasing resources for child protection agencies is critical to reducing the time that children spend unnecessarily in out-of-home care.

Adequate Child Welfare Staffing

Caseworkers are responsible for coordinating efforts to reunite families, documenting those efforts, and working toward a permanent placement for each child. Excessive caseloads increase delays in permanency planning for children. Delays in identifying children for adoption grow even longer because of the considerable caseworker time required to prepare each case for TPR. Overworking the casework staff contributes heavily to high turnover rates and large numbers of unfilled positions.

The number of children in foster care is growing in most states. Agency staffing must keep pace with the growing number of children who need protective intervention. For states to meet the goals of federal foster care law—that a permanent plan for each child be achieved after 18 months in care—caseloads must be reduced by increasing the caseworker and supervisory staff and adding a permanency planning specialist to each staff, together with paralegal and clerical support people.

Family Preservation and Reunification Services

A focus on support services for families is essential to the goals of permanency planning. An adequate array of high-quality preventive services, especially intensive home-based services, will reduce the number of children who enter foster care. Readily available reunification services will enhance an agency's ability to return foster children to their families. When these services are not provided, or there are long waiting lists before such services can be offered, children spend time in out-of-home care unnecessarily.

Lack of services not only results in children staying in care too long before they can return home but also delays the decision to terminate parental rights where that is appropriate. The agency usually must establish that it has made efforts to reunify the family before a court will permit termination of parental rights. When the service history is inadequate, due to underfunding of services, the loser is the child.

Attorneys for the Department

Adequate, competent, and zealous legal advocacy for the agency is a key element in reducing delays in termination of parental rights cases. Attorneys are critical at every stage of a child protection case, but especially when terminating parental rights. Without enough attorneys to represent the department, TPR cases are often pushed to the back burner, as other emergency hearings and hearings with established time limits take priority. In-depth attorney involvement early in a case can help the department identify potential legal obstacles to TPR. For example, the attorney may evaluate the need to involve a putative father in the case plan and point out where the department's reunification efforts have to be strengthened.

The size of attorney caseloads can significantly affect the quality of legal representation that a department obtains. Segal [1988] describes 40 to 50 active child welfare cases as a reasonable caseload for a full-time attorney, fewer than 40 as preferable, and more than 60 as unmanageable.

Handling long and complex TPR trials creates serious problems when not enough attorney time is devoted to child welfare cases. Plea bargaining at the TPR stage, necessitated by staff shortages and limited court time, usually extends the amount of time children remain without a permanent home. More attorneys are needed to represent child welfare departments in foster care cases.

Getting Started

We hope that this chapter has given readers some ideas for tackling problems in their own agencies that keep children in foster care limbo. Despite resource shortages, dedicated staff members, good communications, and concerted efforts can still accomplish a great deal. Outside help is available. Copies of the materials developed for the project and information on legal training and technical assistance are available on request from Debra Ratterman, State Training Director, ABA Center on Children and the Law, 1800 M Street, NW, Washington, DC 20036, (202) 331–2672. The TPR checklist developed for New York State follows, as an example for other jurisdictions.

Bibliography: ABA Center on Children and the Law Termination Barriers Project

American Bar Association. *New Jersey Project on Special Needs Adoption* (June 11, 1985).

American Bar Association (ABA). *1988 Update to the New Jersey Project on Special Needs Adoption.* Washington, DC: ABA, January 20, 1989.

American Bar Association (ABA). *Protecting Children through the Legal System.* Washington, DC: ABA, 1981.

American Bar Association, et. al. *Strengthening Adoption Opportunities in New Jersey: The Northern Regional Report* (July 1987).

Cox, M. and Cox, R. *Foster Care: Current Issues, Policies, and Practices.* Norwood, NJ: Ablex, 1985.

Cunningham, C., and Horowitz, B. *Child Abuse and Neglect: Cases, Text and Problems.* Washington, DC: American Bar Association, 1989.

Cunningham, C., and Horowitz, B. *Handling Child Abuse and Neglect Cases.* Washington, DC: American Bar Association, 1989.

Dodson, D. *The Legal Framework for Ending Foster Care Drift.* Washington, DC: American Bar Association, 1983.

Downs, S., and Taylor, C. *Permanent Planning in Foster Care: Resources for Training.* Portland, OR: Regional Research Institute for Human Services, 1978.

Hardin, M., and Shalleck, A. *Court Rules to Achieve Permanency for Foster Children.* Washington, DC: American Bar Association, 1985.

Hardin, M., ed. *Foster Children in the Courts.* Boston: Butterworth Legal Publishers, 1983.

Hardin, M. "Legal Representation of Child Welfare Agencies." *Legal Response: Child Advocacy and Protection* (Winter and Spring 1983).

Hardin, M. *Termination of Parental Rights: A Summary and Comparison of Grounds from Nine Model Acts.* Washington, DC: National Legal Resource Center for Child Advocacy and Protection, American Bar Association, 1981.

Horowitz, R. and Davidson, H. *Legal Rights of Children* (1984 and Supplement 1988) Washington, DC: American Bar Association.

Kadushin, A. *Child Welfare Services,* 3rd. ed. New York: Macmillan, 1980.

Konigsberg, K. *Ties That Bind: State Termination of Parental Rights, Preventing Harm to the Child.* 1989.

Laird, J., and Hartman, A, eds. *A Handbook of Child Welfare: Context, Knowledge, and Practice.* New York: The Free Press, 1985.

Mid-Hudson Regional Legal Conference. *Working for Permanency: The Family Court and the Department of Social Services.* 1988.

National Conference of State Legislatures (NCSL). *Child Welfare in the States: Fifty State Survey Report.* Denver, CO: NCSL, 1986.

New York Task Force on Permanency Planning for Children in Foster Care. *Permanency Planning: A Shared Responsibility.* March 1986.

Ratterman, D. *Child Welfare Legal Manual for DSS Caseworkers* Washington, DC: National Legal Resource Center for Child Advocacy and Protection, American Bar Association, 1990.

Ratterman, D. *Child Welfare Legal Manual for DSS Attorneys and Law Guardians.* Washington, DC: National Legal Resource Center for Child Advocacy and Protection, American Bar Association, 1988 and 1990 Supplement.

Reiniger, D. "Freeing Children for Adoption: Termination of Parental Rights." In *Child Abuse and Neglect: Protecting the Child, Defending the Parent, Representing the State.* New York: Practicing Law Institute, 1988.

Segal, E. *Evaluating and Improving Child Welfare Agency Legal Representation.* Washington, DC: National Legal Resource Center for Child Advocacy and Protection, American Bar Association, 1988.

In the Matter of Sheila G. 61 N. Y. 2d 368, 462 N. E. 2d 1139, 462 N. Y. S. 2d 1139 (1984).

Spinak, Jane. *Permanency Planning Judicial Benchbook.* Albany, NY: Unified Court System, 1989.

Whittaker, J.; Kinney, J.; Tracy, E.; and Booth, C. *Improving Practice Technology for Work with High Risk Families: Lessons from the Homebuilders Social Work Education Project.* Seattle: University of Washington Center for Social Welfare Research, 1988.

*New York State Termination Checklist**

Termination Checklist

Instructions: Once the decision has been made that it is appropriate to begin a termination proceeding, use the following checklist to make sure that all the necessary information is in the case file in preparation for review by the county attorney. The completed checklist can be used to prepare the petition for termination of parental rights. This is not a separate form that must be filled out—it simply provides guidelines for preparing a case for termination.

Case Name _____ **Case No.** _____ **Date** _____

1. Family Information

a. Child's name: _____

    Date of birth: _____ Place of birth: _____

    Birth certificate in file?   Yes _____   No _____

b. Mother's name: _____ Age: _____

    Address: _____

    If the mother's address is unknown, complete the Missing Parent Checklist.

c. Father's name: _____ Age: _____

    Address: _____

    If the father's address is unknown, complete the Missing Parent Checklist.

    If the child who is the subject of the termination is nonmarital (born out of wedlock), complete the following checklist:

(1) Consent Father

❏ (a) Child under six months old
  ❏ Father lived with child or child's mother for continuous six months prior to placement.
  ❏ Father openly held himself out as the child's father six months prior to placement.
  ❏ Father paid or offered to pay a fair and reasonable sum toward medical expenses of birth.

❏ (b) Child over six months old
  ❏ Father pays child support.
  ❏ Father visits child monthly or regularly contacts child.
  ❏ Father physically able to contact child.
  ❏ Father not prevented from contacting child.

❏ (c) Father lived with the child six months in the one-year period prior to placement.
  ❏ Father openly held himself out as the child's father.

If an unwed father meets all the conditions of (a), (b), or (c) above, he is a consent father and the child may not be adopted unless the father's parental rights have been surrendered or terminated. If the unwed father does not meet the requirements of a consent father, complete the following section:

(2) Notice Father

❏ (a) Father was adjudicated to be the father of the child in a New York court.
  Order in file? Yes _____ No _____

* Note: This document is a confidential attorney/client communication. As such, it should be kept in a separate file marked "confidential and privileged communications" and not be made available for review by any other party.

New York State Termination Checklist (cont.)

☐ (b) Father was adjudicated to be the father of the child in an out-of-state court.
    ☐ Order was filed with putative father registry.

☐ (c) Father filed a notice of intent to claim paternity.

☐ (d) Father is named on child's birth certificate.

☐ (e) Father lived with the child or the child's mother at the time of placement.
    ☐ Father openly held himself out as the child's father.

☐ (f) Father was identified as the child's father by mother in a sworn, written statement.

☐ (g) Father was married to mother within six months after the child's birth.
    ☐ Father married mother prior to the execution of a surrender or initiation of termination.

☐ (h) Father filed with putative father registry.

If the unwed father meets any of the requirements of (a), (b), (c), (d),(e),(f),(g) or (h), he must be notified of any action to voluntarily place the child, surrender the child, or terminate the mother's parental rights. He may only offer evidence concerning the best interest of the child at the disposition hearing. His rights do not have to be terminated or surrendered for the child to be adopted, as long as he is given notice. If an unwed father does not meet any of these requirements, he does not have a right to be heard or notified of a termination action or adoption of the child.

2. Termination Grounds

    a. Death

	Mother	Father
(1) Death of both parents		
(2) No guardian appointed		
b. Abandonment		
(1) Child in care for six months	___	___
(2) During the last six months, the parent:		
(a) Failed to visit child and	___	___
(b) Failed to communicate with child and	___	___
(c) Failed to contact the agency	___	___
(3) Parent physically and financially able	___	___
(4) Not discouraged or prevented by agency	___	___
c. Permanent Neglect		
(1) Child in care for one year	___	___
(2) During a one-year period, the parent:		
(a) Failed to maintain contact with child or	___	___
(b) Failed to plan for future of child	___	___
(3) Parent physically and financially able	___	___
(4) Not discouraged or prevented by agency	___	___

New York State Termination Checklist (cont.)

	Mother	Father
(5) Diligent efforts		
(a) Were made to reunify the family		___
(b) Were detrimental to child		___
(c) Parent failed to keep agency apprised of their location for at least six months.		___
(d) Incarcerated parent failed on more than one occasion to cooperate with the agency on visitation or planning. See the Diligent Efforts Affidavit Format.		___
d. Mental Illness or Mental Retardation		
(1) Child in care for one year	___	___
(2) Parent is mentally ill or	___	___
(3) Parent is mentally retarded or	___	___
(4) Unable to care for child for the foreseeable future		

Expert(s) who evaluated parent:

Name: _____

Qualifications: _____

Date of Evaluation: _____

Reports in file?   Yes _____   No _____

Mother | Father

e. Severe or Repeated Abuse

(1) Child in care for one year _____ _____

(2) Child severely abused or _____ _____

(3) Two adjudications of abuse against parent _____ _____

(4) Diligent efforts

(a) Were made to reunify the family _____ _____

(b) Were detrimental to child _____ _____
See the Diligent Efforts Affidavit Format.

3. **Placement History**

a. Placement with the Department

(1) Date child placed with department: _____

(2) Type of placement:
Abuse _____ Neglect _____ Voluntary _____

(3) Original reason for placement: _____
_____
_____

New York State Termination Checklist (cont.)

b. Child's Current Placement:

Name: _____

Address: _____

Relationship to Child: _____

Dates of Placement: _____ to present

c. Child's Prior Foster Placements

Name: _____

Address: _____

Relationship to Child: _____

Dates of Placement: _____ to _____

Name: _____

Address: _____

Relationship to Child: _____

Dates of Placement: _____ to _____

d. Assigned Caseworkers:

Name: _____

Supervisor: _____

Dates of Assignment: _____ to _____

Name: _____

Supervisor: _____

Dates of Assignment: _____ to _____

Name: _____
Supervisor: _____
Dates of Assignment: _____ to _____

Name: _____
Supervisor: _____
Dates of Assignment: _____ to _____

e. Service Plans

Copies of all service plans in file?   Yes _____   No _____
Copies of all UCR's in file?   Yes _____   No _____

4. Legal History

a. Prior Orders: Briefly summarize the legal history of the case by noting the orders issued by the judge. For abuse and neglect cases these orders may include an emergency placement order, a temporary removal order, a disposition order, and extensions of placement. For voluntary placements, these orders might include judicial approval of the placement instrument and foster care reviews.

_____ Date _____

_____

_____

_____

_____

Copies of orders in file?   Yes _____   No _____

New York State Termination Checklist (cont.)

b. Prior Termination Actions

Has a previous termination action been filed against

Mother? Yes _____ No _____
Date filed: _____ Docket Number: _____
Result: _____
Copies of petition and order in file? Yes _____ No _____

Father? Yes _____ No _____
Date filed: _____ Docket Number: _____
Result: _____
Copies of petition and order in file? Yes _____ No _____

c. Surrenders

(1) Has a surrender been executed by either parent?

Mother? Yes _____ No _____ Date executed: _____
Judicially approved? Yes _____ No _____ Date: _____
Validly revoked? Yes _____ No _____
Copy of surrender
and order in file? Yes _____ No _____

Father? Yes _____ No _____ Date executed: _____
Judicially approved? Yes _____ No _____ Date: _____
Validly revoked? Yes _____ No _____
Copy of surrender
and order in file? Yes _____ No _____

(2) Have both parents been approached to sign a surrender?

Mother? Yes _____ No _____
Willing _____ Refused _____

Father? Yes _____ No _____
Willing _____ Refused _____

5. Child's Status

a. Native American Status**

(1) Is the child a member or eligible to be a member of an Indian tribe?
Yes _____ No _____

(2) Tribal Affiliation:

Mother's tribe: _____
Father's tribe: _____

** Note: If the child is Native American, special requirements of the Indian Child Welfare Act apply to the termination proceedings: (1) notification of the termination must be given to the child's tribe; (2) the agency must show "active efforts" to reunify the family with an emphasis on culturally appropriate services; (3) the agency must show that the child is in danger of serious emotional or physical damage if returned to the parent; and (4) the agency must prove its case for termination "beyond a reasonable doubt." If these special requirements are not met, the termination can be invalidated.

New York State Termination Checklist (cont.)

(3) Notice of Tribe

Has the tribe been notified of the child's placement with the department?

Yes _____ No _____

Date of Notice: _____ Proceedings: _____

Copy of notice in file? Yes _____ No _____

(4) Tribe's Legal Intervention

Has the tribe requested, accepted, or declined custody of the child?

Yes _____ No _____

Date of Notice: _____ Proceedings: _____

Copy of notice in file? Yes _____ No _____

b. Special Needs or Disabilities

Does the child have any disabilities or special needs?

No _____ Yes _____

☐ physical: _____
☐ mental: _____
☐ emotional: _____
☐ other: _____

c. Prospects for Adoption

Assured _____ Excellent _____ Good _____ Fair _____ Poor _____

Potential Adoptive Family:

Name: _____

Address: _____

Relationship to Child: _____

d. Child's Preference

Have you discussed termination and adoption with the child?

Yes _____ No _____

Child's response: _____

_____

_____

_____

_____

_____

_____

_____

Does the child oppose adoption?   Yes _____ No _____

Is the child over 14 years of age?   Yes _____ No _____

CHAPTER 4

Effective Practices: Changing a System to Change a Child's Life

Betsy Farley

Jim is 23 years old, a paramedic, and happy with his life. Becoming a productive, happy adult has not been easy for Jim, and his experience has not been typical. As a young child, he was severely abused and neglected by his family. As his family problems escalated, so did his acting out. When Jim was 10, the Kentucky Department for Social Services initiated termination of parental rights (TPR) procedures. The search for an adoptive home began when he was 12 and ended when he was 14.

The Department for Social Services, like most child welfare agencies, considers TPR in only the small percentage of cases where all available interventions have failed to provide a safe, secure, nurturing, and stable home. Jim's case reflects a troubling but common situation—the TPR process was not initiated until the child had spent years in and out of foster homes, and the bureaucratic system took too long to follow through. Jim will tell you today that his life is better because he was adopted, but he will also tell you that his feelings about the process are fraught with uncertainty, anxiety, anger, frustration, and guilt. These feelings are sometimes directed at the system, sometimes at his family, and sometimes at himself.

He is very close to his adoptive family, but occasionally he sees his biological mother. This contact has helped him work through some of his feelings. He talks about wishing the adoption could have happened earlier and faster, so that it wouldn't have taken so long to know where he was going to live and if he would be staying in the same school. Most important, adoption would have given him the family he wanted sooner.

Jim's case is a good illustration of why Kentucky decided to improve the TPR process. A child who has been severely abused or neglected usually has problems developing and growing up normally; any child who is not living in a permanent home is likely to find growing up difficult. Once the decision is made to free a child for adoption, the case should be expedited. All the professionals involved should know the process for terminating parents' rights and make sure that the case keeps the child's needs clearly in focus and proceeds without unnecessary delays.

In the following pages, the approach and outcome of Kentucky's Termination of Parental Rights (TPR) project are presented and discussed. It was a process that involved a blue ribbon committee to review state statutes, policies, and procedures; to take the responsibility for initiating changes; and to establish a tracking system to ensure that changes would be permanent.

The Approach

As has been stated previously in this book, reviewing and evaluating the TPR process in state and county systems is critical to providing vulnerable children with an opportunity to grow up safe, happy, and loved. Unfortunately, the bureaucratic legal process often allows the needs of the system to take priority over the child's needs. When this happens, it follows inevitably that the system does not act in an efficient, timely, or child-sensitive manner.

The professionals involved in processing TPR cases agree that the process takes too long. Some of the reasons are obvious—the complexity of the cases, an overburdened system (growing numbers of cases, but no growth in the numbers of judges, lawyers, or social workers to handle them), and the system's reluctance to dissolve the bonds of family—but none of them change the central fact. Every child has a right to a safe, permanent, and nurturing home. When a jurisdiction makes a priority of the child's right to a safe and permanent home, policies, procedures, and priorities will and do change.

That premise, and an interagency, cooperative effort using a centralized approach underlay this project of the Kentucky Department for Social Services. The department collaborated with seven other agencies and organizations in applying for a grant from the Office of Human Development Services. An advisory committee of 13 members, representing social services, the courts, attorneys, the legislature, and advocacy groups, was appointed by the secretary of the cabinet to evaluate the problem, recommend solutions, and monitor changes. The committee was supported by the staff of the Department for Social Services, the Office of Counsel in the Cabinet for Human Resources, and the Administrative Office of the Courts. The chair of the committee was a chief judge of the Circuit Court. The committee was divided and expanded into five subcommittees: legislative, social services, courts, training, and video development. The project was designed to ensure input from all levels of workers and all parties to the proceedings.

One expert from the American Bar Association and another from the Oregon Children's Services Division helped with the needs assessment. The consultant from Oregon worked with the committee throughout the project, providing insight and objectivity as recommendations were developed and plans implemented.

A systems management approach known as *strategic planning* was adapted for use with this project, which had four principal phases: assessment, development of action plans, implementation of the plans, and evaluation and follow-up.

Strategic planning has become a popular management technique because its principles are based on informed, shared decision-making and consensus formation, and its outcomes focus on taking responsibility for action. The underlying assumptions are that people want to participate in decisions that affect them and that they will support what they create. The process also assumes that two minds are better than one, as long as actions or outcomes remain doable.

The action-planning process has three components: problem identification, problem solution, and planning. The process involves seven steps.

1. Describe the problem.
2. List the issues.
3. Establish priorities and select those for the action plan.
4. Determine how to deal with the problem.

5. Select activities.

6. Identify resources and impediments.

7. Focus on the solution.

The first three steps were completed by the advisory committee during its first six months of operation. Each subcommittee developed an action plan by using the seven steps. There were three primary subcommittees: Cabinet for Human Resources, Courts, and Legislation. Two additional subcommittees were formed to work on the video and training portion of the project. Each subcommittee submitted its plan to the full committee for approval before embarking on implementation.

Background Information

The following section offers a review of Kentucky's TPR process, the status of the TPR cases found at the beginning of the project, and the initial recommendations of the advisory committee.

Social Services

The Kentucky Department for Social Services (DSS) is one of six departments within the Cabinet for Human Resources. The cabinet has established an Office of Counsel whose attorneys are assigned to regions throughout the state and represent the cabinet in TPR proceedings. The Division of Family Services is the administrative unit responsible for child protection, foster care, and adoption. Programs are administered by the central office through 14 district offices and 128 local offices.

Kentucky's Department for Social Services is committed to a services approach that focuses on families rather than individuals. Services in this context are intended to strengthen and maintain families and to prevent family breakdown and out-of-home placement. The department helps families to maintain or regain family autonomy while assuring protection for children. When children cannot be protected or their needs cannot be met at home, they are separated from the parents and placed in a relative's home, a family foster home, or another appropriate placement.

The Legal Process

A child who enters Kentucky's foster care system is first committed by the state district court to the Cabinet for Human Resources and placed in out-of-home care. The cabinet social worker begins making plans for a permanent living arrangement for the child. The biological family is, under most circumstances, provided with various social services for up to six months, at which point an administrative review is held to evaluate progress on the case plan. At this time a decision is usually made about what is best for the child. If conditions in the child's own home have improved, the plan may be to return the child to his or her biological parents. In other circumstances, the state may continue the child's placement in permanent out-of-home care or prepare the child for independent living. If necessary, the cabinet can pursue TPR, and ultimately, adoption.

If the chosen plan is involuntary TPR and subsequent adoption, the worker consults with the cabinet's Office of Counsel on pursuing a TPR decision and supplies information on why it is needed. The office attorney draws up a petition for involuntary TPR that the worker files in the county circuit court. A local attorney is appointed by the court to represent the child's best interests as her or his guardian ad litem. Attorneys may be appointed for the parents also. Various other legal processes take place before the day of the hearing. At the hearing, the cabinet is charged with the responsibility of proving, by clear and convincing evidence, that TPR is in the best interests of the child. After the hearing, the judge makes the final decision. Either party has the right to appeal the judge's decision to the Kentucky Court of Appeals.

At the time this project began, the child protective services manual listed 16 steps for workers to follow, from the starting point of consulting with the Office of Counsel through the preparation of the presentation summary. Figure 1 summarizes this process.

Project Data

Data Collection

The Systems Administration Branch, Kentucky's centralized unit to coordinate, collect, control, and computerize statewide information for the Department for Social Services, designed an automated tracking system for TPR cases. Developing the tracking system was to be a high priority during the startup of the project,

Figure 1. Kentucky's TPR Process before the Project

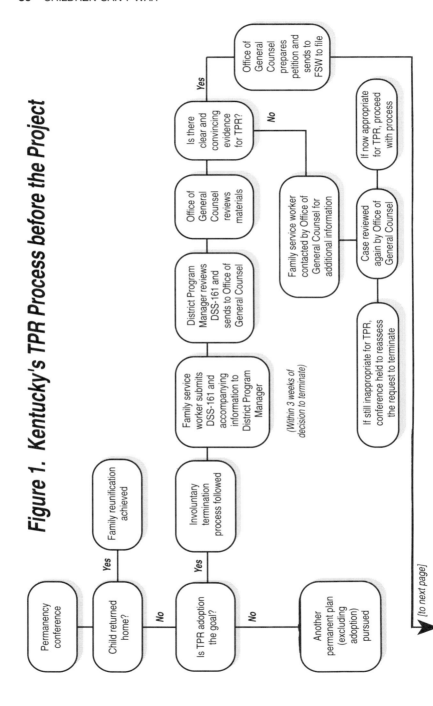

[to next page]

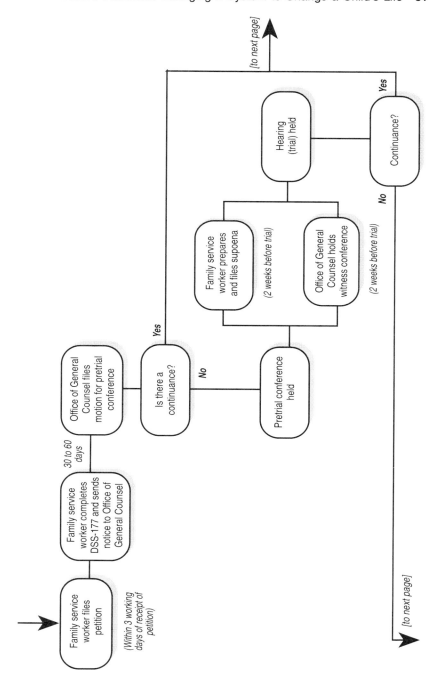

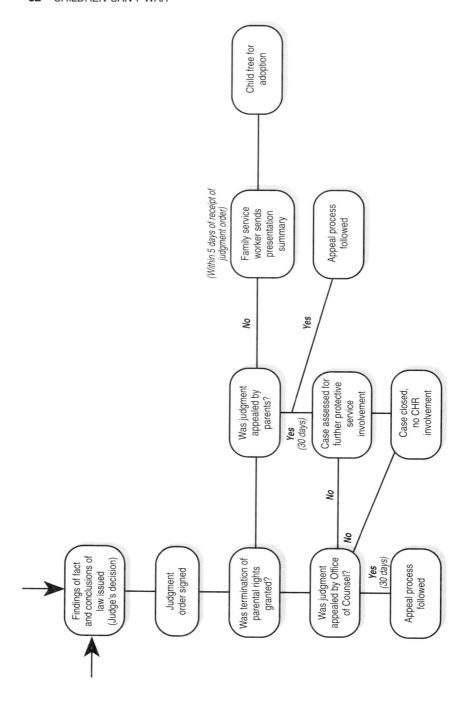

but two new developments caused the time frame to be delayed and the approach to be expanded.

The first was a consent decree from a District Court judge that required the cabinet to monitor and report on permanency planning for children in foster care and demonstrate that the intent of P.L. 96–272 was being implemented in Jefferson County, the major metropolitan area of the state. A stand-alone computer tracking system that was operating in that county at the time the project began had served as a pilot project for the statewide system. It was determined that a statewide system should not be implemented until the consent decree ended or appropriate adjustments could be made in the system.

The second change arose over the number of separate tracking systems being developed to collect data. At the time the project was initiated, there were six separate systems. The committee recommended developing one coordinated system; DSS agreed to make this major adjustment and allocated money and staff to do it.

This change in approach significantly altered the way that baseline data would be collected, and these data were needed before the advisory committee could develop the action plans. The committee decided to review all appellate court cases and a 10% random sample of TPR cases for one year, noting seven dates when action should take place but delays could occur. Then the Office of Counsel began collecting data for all TPR cases initiated during the next fiscal year, FY '90. Finally, a special computer program was written to obtain selected data on cases in which a formal request for TPR was made by the staff to the Office of General Counsel for three consecutive years, FY '89 through FY '91. These three sources yielded the database the committee would use to develop its plans and to make final recommendations. The following sections of this chapter discuss the data and the action plans of the three primary subcommittees and summarize their resulting activities.

Findings

From July 1, 1987, through June 30, 1990, TPR proceedings were initiated that involved 753 children. This is an average of 251 children a year, approximately 4% of those who entered family foster care and slightly more than 1% of the number of substantiated reports of abused and neglected children. The number of substantiated reports and the number of children who entered foster care continued to increase, but the number of children involved in TPR and their age distribution remained relatively constant. Sixty percent of these children were under three, 51% were ages four through 12, and 5% were over 13. Only .01% were 17 years of age.

Fifty-five percent of the children were boys and 45% were girls. 74% were white, 21% were black, and 4% were Hispanic. Two Asian children and one Native American child were also involved in TPR during this three-year period. In relation to state statistics on the racial composition of reported cases, the ratio of black children involved in TPR outnumbered white children. Ten percent of all the children were reported to have physical handicaps, and 31% had emotional problems. Fifty-four percent of the children were part of sibling groups. The primary reason for placement was neglect (49% of cases), followed by abuse (13%), parental incapacity (12%), sexual abuse (7%), voluntary release for adoption (6%), and abandonment (5%).

The most frequently reported permanency planning goal was adoption. Permanent out-of-home care was the second, but significantly less frequent, goal. Relatively few cases were reported to have independent living as an exiting goal.

Two other figures provide insight on this group of children: their average length of time in care and the average number of placements from the time they entered care until TPR was in process. The average length of time in care fell from 2.8 years in 1988 to 2.0 years in 1990, and the average number of placements went from four to three. Twenty-six children involved in TPR proceedings during this time period had been in care five or more years, but this number significantly decreased in the year following the initiation of this grant project—to 14 in 1988 and to four in 1990.

Limited, but interesting, data provided information on the families for which TPR proceedings were initiated. The average age of parents was 30, and nearly three-quarters of the families were headed by females. More than half the parents were single. The five counties with the highest numbers of TPR cases were Jefferson (31%), Fayette (9%), Kenton (7%), Magoffin (4%), and Warren (3%). The districts with the highest numbers of TPR cases were Jefferson (31%), Bluegrass (15%), and Northern Kentucky (10.5%), the three most densely populated areas of the state. It was found that 36 counties (20% of the total) had not filed any

TPR petitions during the three years of this study, and another 11% had filed only one TPR case during the three-year period.

Evaluating Kentucky's TPR Process

In addition to obtaining an objective picture of the children and families who were involved in TPR, it was critical to understand how well the process was working. It was particularly important to determine at which steps delays occurred and how long they were taking. A 10% random survey was done of all children for whom a decision had been reached or a decision was pending during FY '88. Thirty-one cases were reviewed by the child protection service specialists in each district. After a review and pilot test of the initial tracking document, seven time periods were identified for measurement and documentation. In table 1, the mean, range, and median are given for the times that elapsed from step to step.

The total average time that children waited from the point when the goal became adoption until the TPR process was complete was two years and two months at the beginning of the project. At the end of the project this time had been shortened to just under one year and two months.

Some additional information that was elicited is not reflected in the chart. In more than a quarter of the cases, the social workers filed the petition in circuit court the same day that they received it. In more than a third of the cases, it took longer than 12 months from the time the petition was filed to the trial date. In two-fifths of the cases, the judge made an entry of judgment on the day when the trial concluded.

Tracking TPR Activities in FY '89

The Appeals Process

All TPR cases that were appealed during the one-year period of September 1988 through August 1989 were reviewed for time delays. The total was ten cases, with ten points of action identified from date of judgment to the date when opinions were issued and reviewed for potential delay. Table 2 is a summary of a typical case, which took just over a year.

Table 1. Cases Decided or Pending Decision during FY 1988

From	To	Mean	Range	Median
Permanency conference	Worker requests TPR (DSS 161)	1.5 months	2 days to 10 months	3.5 weeks
Worker request	Worker receives petition to file	2 months	1 week to 18 months	4 weeks
Petition received by worker	Worker files petition in court	6 days	same day to 1 month	2 days
Petition filed	Trial date	12.7 months	3 months to 31 months	40 weeks
Trial date	Judge's decision	1.8 months	same day to 10 months	same day
Judge's decision	Entry of judgment	5.5 days	same day to 2 months	same day
Signing of judgment order	Sending presentation summary	1 month	same day to 5 months	2 weeks

---

Table 2. Summary of Typical Case, 1989-'90

1. Date of Judgment 4/17/89
   Notice of Appeal (30 days allowed): 5/13/89

2. Notice of Appeal 5/13/89
   Prehearing statement (14 days): 6/14/89

3. Prehearing statement 6/14/89
   Prehearing conference order: 7/17/89

4. Prehearing conference order 7/17/89
   Circuit court record certified (30 days allowed video,
   60 days allowed written record): 9/15/89

5. Circuit court record certified 9/15/89
   Appellant brief (30 days allowed): 10/13/89

6. Appellant brief 11/13/89
   Apellant brief (30 days allowed): 11/13/89

7. Appellant brief 11/13/89
   Record filed (no times after this point): 1/24/90

8. Record filed 1/25/90
   Assigned 2/16/90 (judge given 6 weeks to prepare,
   until 4/90)

9. Assigned 4/90

10. Opinion 5/4/90

The appellate judge who conducted the review concluded that the review process took so long partly because TPR cases were handled in the same manner as other cases. In appeals filed on TPR cases in Kentucky, insufficiency of evidence is most often cited as the reason for the appeal, and reversals are usually due to the agency's not having used procedural alternatives before initiating the TPR. He recommended eliminating the prehearing conference phase and adding a priority assignment to TPR cases, developing a special designation for TPR motions that would shorten the time below the four months common at that time, and waiving oral arguments except upon request by one of two parties involved.

These recommendations were acted on. The appellate judge and two other Kentucky Appeals Court judges have agreed to serve on a special panel to hear TPR cases. This will enable an opinion to be rendered more efficiently—in many cases, within six months—saving 50% of the time previously required to review cases.

Case Reviews and Comments

Ideas were sought from many sources on what problems were encountered during the TPR process and what changes could improve the system. The comments that follow illustrate the type of information that provided insight for the committee.

A consultant to the project

> The cardinal issues are: should the child suffer, and if so, for how long? From my perspective, being fully cognizant of the importance of the family, we are causing suffering and we are waiting too long to change the goal to adoption. More than 8% of the children we are placing for adoption have suffered irrevocable mental, emotional, or physical injury and will require special, intense, structured parenting. The more comprehensive and complex the child's problems, the more difficult it becomes to recruit an appropriate adoptive home and the greater the postadoptive services that will be required to sustain that placement.

Bluegrass District staff member

> One may believe that establishing a goal that involves TPR would reduce the demands on the worker, but this is not the case. Service provision that includes visiting to these families is maintained, if not intensified, when the goal is changed. Paperwork demands and extraneous clerical chores also intensify. At times it requires the assistance of all office staff to accomplish what is expected.

An adoptive parent

Not only was it hard to find informed professionals to assist us through the TPR process, but we also found that the separate agencies and individuals involved did not overlap services well and truly did not know each other's jobs and limitations. Trying to stay within, or even find, the laws governing what we were doing became more than frustrating. We would love for more people dealing with cases such as this to be well informed and prepared to assist all the parties involved. It would be nice if the courts and the cabinet had a closer working relationship and knowledge of each other's limitations. We would love for the laws of Kentucky to begin to protect our children rather than always protecting the rights of the biological parents.

An adopted youth

It is a process. TPR takes a lot of time, and it is not the best process, but you know in life it has to be done. A lot of times it's a long period of time before a child can be put with adoptive parents and everything. It's really hard on a child dealing with being between homes and not knowing where they stand and everything like that. It makes it real hard on a child. Like when I was taken away from my mother, I didn't know who was coming to get me. I didn't know why they'd come to get me. All I knew was that they came in my home and took me away from my mother, which was the only thing I knew.

Purchase District staff member

Attorneys have too many cases. They do a good job; we are not complaining about them. But why should it take eight months to get a hearing set? It seems we (DSS staff) break our necks to get all our paperwork completed and then just sit and wait. On another case, we had a TPR hearing October 25th. The judge said he was going to terminate the parents' rights. We received the order on December 19th for the judge's signature. It took two months to write up the order; the attorneys must have too many responsibilities.

A Chief Circuit Court judge

> Next to death penalty criminal cases, termination of parental rights cases are probably the most serious decisions we make.

The Assistant General Counsel, Cabinet for Human Resources

> Some guardians ad litem will take a case very seriously, interviewing the child, looking at the record, calling witnesses. Others will simply appear in court and offer their opinion.

A youth whose TPR case has been appealed

> A judge should consider everybody's side, not just the adults'. My mom and dad have had so many chances. Who makes more difference than the judge? He makes the decision. I would like for my judge to listen to me. My judge has gone too far with my parents. Seven years is too long; I'm only 13.

Comments such as these gave the committee an insight and focus that continued throughout the project. The committee made efforts to listen to all parties involved in the cases, including children, young adults, parents, and workers who waited for TPR proceedings to be complete so that the goal of adoption could be pursued.

Initial Legislative Recommendations

Following the needs assessment, the committee voted on initial recommendations, established the three primary subcommittees, developed action plans, and initiated the implementation phase. Its recommendations are summarized as follows:

- Amend the putative father statute;
- Decrease the waiting period for petitions on abandoned children;
- Give the court discretion to appoint a guardian ad litem in voluntary TPR cases;
- Address delivery of social services immediately before and after filing petitions;

- Grant the court authority to terminate parental visiting after petition if it is found to be detrimental to the child.

Reports of the Primary Subcommittees

Human Resources Subcommittee

Goal

To review policy and procedures within the cabinet that affect permanence for children.

Objectives

1. To review the TPR chapter of the DSS Policy and Procedures Manual.

   The TPR chapter was found to be difficult to understand, and some procedures required by the manual involved unnecessary time delays. These policies and procedures were reviewed by staff members familiar with the TPR process to simplify and expedite this process.

2. To examine the absent-parent search process.

   It was clear that the process incurred delays, largely because it was a time-consuming task that received lower priority than the daily crises child protective services workers faced. The actual search was largely clerical, and was unfamiliar to most of the workers, who rarely went through the process. It was also noted that the workers rarely completed a search when a child entered care, waiting instead until a TPR action was underway. The manual has been revised to encourage completion of the absent-parent search when a child enters care. A handbook was also created to help staff members conduct the search effectively.

3. To review the process and forms used by DSS staff to initiate TPR with the Office of Counsel.

   The preparation of the case information for the Office of Counsel was found to be difficult and cumbersome, involving writing a chronology of the entire case and completing several repetitive forms. The format of case information requested by the Office of Counsel was revised to simplify the process and more closely reflect the evidential needs of the case.

4. To develop a statewide automated system for tracking children involved in TPR.

    The existing system for tracking children in out-of-home care was found to be inaccurate and lacking necessary detail. It also failed to track the individual steps within the TPR process. A new automated system was designed to document a child's progress from entering out-of-home care through achieving a permanency goal. Tracking each step means that compliance with established time frames is monitored and management reports are sent to each district office. This system has been well accepted by the staff because it combined a number of existing systems and reduced the number of forms staff members had to prepare.

5. To inform all parents of the possibility of termination when a child enters care.

    A statement was designed for inclusion in the out-of-home care treatment plan informing parents that TPR is an option for achieving permanence for children.

6. To examine methods to improve communication between the DSS staff and the Office of Counsel.

    It was decided that many delays arose because staff members identified a case for termination of parental rights before all the legal grounds were met and the evidential issues resolved. Improving communication between the Office of Counsel and the field staff brought about the development of a step called the prepermanency planning conference. This conference, in which workers review a case with attorneys before making a decision to change the goal to adoption, was the only additional step recommended. It has been used across the state for nearly a year, and is described by staff members as highly effective in reducing delays.

Summary

The TPR Advisory Committee recommended that these changes be implemented through normal policy and procedural changes; however, a training session was held for district staff that emphasized not only the policy changes but also the importance of working toward permanence from the department's first contact with the child and family. The committee also recommended that district managers assign district-level clerical workers to access the Kentucky Information Systems and conduct all absent-parent searches within the district, developing an expertise in conducting searches quickly and efficiently and lessening the burden on field workers.

It was further recommended that the data collected from the out-of-home tracking system be regularly reviewed and reports submitted to the director's office. This review, conducted by the data systems branch with the assistance of the Children and Youth Services Branch, identifies continuing points of delay.

Courts Subcommittee

Goal

To identify delays in court procedures in TPR cases and recommend appropriate policy and procedural changes to reduce delays.

Objectives

1. To provide educational resources for legal professionals.

    Two newsletters have been developed on the child's right to permanence and the TPR project's objectives. Time delays were identified and discussed in the newsletter. The newsletters were mailed to all circuit and appellate judges, all attorneys who received fees as appointed guardians ad litem, parents' attorneys, the DSS staff, foster care review boards, and court-appointed special advocates. The *Children Can't Wait* videotape was produced to sensitize all professionals to the needs of children. Four one-day seminars were conducted on the effects of delays in the TPR process. One of these seminars was developed exclusively for circuit judges.

Effects

These initiatives have informed officers of the court of the need to proceed expeditiously with TPR cases for the child's benefit. Attorneys and judges have been advised of recommended policy and statutory changes and updates of current case law, and have increased their understanding of the child's point of view in the TPR process.

2. To pursue training for guardians ad litem.

    The committee reviewed the process of appointing guardians ad litem and paying for their services. Three one-day regional seminars were held for a multidisciplinary audience on the effects of delays on children and the TPR process.

Effects

The review of the current system of appointing and compensating guardians ad litem revealed practice inconsistencies throughout the state. Committee members agreed that specific training should be required for those who accept guardian ad litem appointments. This would ensure adequate representation for the child during the TPR hearing (see further discussion under Recommendations). The regional seminars would provide continuing Legal Education Units for guardian ad litem training.

3. To examine court rules.

TPR statutes and related rules of court were reviewed. Legislative and policy changes were recommended. The Court of Appeals has instituted a system of special designation for TPR cases and appointed a special panel to review all TPR appeals.

Effects

The legislative recommendations urge that TPR cases be heard within 60 days of a request for a trial date; that the period of time for abandonment as grounds be shortened from six months to three months; and that the court render a decision within 30 days of the hearing. The recommendations, if enacted by the General Assembly, would create specific time frames for actions and decisions, thus eliminating periods of waiting. The Supreme Court submission rule would be modified from 90 days to 30 days. The initiatives of the Court of Appeals should significantly reduce the time frames for appeals from an average of two years to six months.

4. To update and revise the bench book for circuit judges.

The current edition of the bench book has been revised to include current case law and expanded explanations of the TPR process and statutory requirements.

Effects

Judges now have immediate access to process and case law pertaining to TPR hearings. This section of the bench book had not been revised since 1985.

Recommendations

1. Further reviewing the guardian ad litem system.

   An interagency study group composed of representatives from the Finance Cabinet, the Cabinet for Human Resources, the Administrative Office of the Courts, the Office of the Attorney General, and the Kentucky Bar Association has been proposed to the Children's Rights Committee of the Kentucky Bar Association. This committee will explore contracting for guardian services to assure greater expertise and control costs. It may be feasible to consider personal service contracts with attorneys who agree to accept a specified number of cases as guardians ad litem or parents' attorneys. This may be done in conjunction with the following objective, training for guardians ad litem.

2. Developing a training curriculum for guardians ad litem.

   The subcommittee wished to recommend that payment for guardian ad litem services be increased for those who had specialized training, but could not forward that recommendation until the training was available. The Office of Attorney General has entered into a contract with the DSS to develop a training curriculum for guardians ad litem. This curriculum was developed and pilot-tested in 1992, and action is being taken to require it for all GALs.

3. Amending the circuit judges' bench book if legislative proposals are enacted.

   As noted above, the Administrative Office of the Courts revised the bench book after the 1992 Kentucky General Assembly to reflect all statutory changes.

4. Supporting further development of the Family Court system in Kentucky.

   During the regional training, several of the small discussion groups identified the judges' unfamiliarity with TPR as a concern. Statistical data revealed that many counties had never heard a TPR case and several had heard only one within the past three years. The Courts Subcommittee supports the continual development of Family Court systems. This would increase the judges' familiarity with children's needs and with standards, services, reasonable efforts, and case law.

   Improvements in handling the TPR cases in the court system depend largely on the quality of advocacy for the child's right to permanence and safety and the sensitivity of the judicial officer hearing the case. This project has influenced both training and production of materials for court officials. Delays have been reduced significantly by the actions of the Court of Appeals, and will be further reduced if the legislative proposals are enacted.

Training for guardians ad litem is difficult, and will require further efforts beyond this project, which has at this point identified several areas of concern and created an impetus for a productive solution.

The Legislative Subcommittee

Goal

To review the Kentucky Revised Statute pertaining to termination of parental rights process and develop recommendations for legislative change.

Objectives

1. To identify the elements of the statute that relate to unnecessary delays in the termination of parental rights process;
2. To review model statutes from other states and case law decisions affecting termination of parental rights.
3. To revise the statute to eliminate unnecessary delays in permanence for children while being sensitive to the rights of parents and/or guardians.

Summary

On the basis of the recommendations of the advisory committee, consultation, and a comprehensive review of Kentucky's termination of parental rights statutes and case law, the subcommittee drafted a revision of the TPR statute. The advisory committee discussed and voted on each recommended change. Briefly stated, the areas of revision are:

1. Legislatively mandating time frames for the conduct of proceedings.

    For instance, it was proposed that the trial in chief be held within 60 days of the filing of the petition and a decision be rendered within 30 days from the close of evidence.
2. Revising the statute to state that the child is a nominal party who is not a respondent to the action, to make clear that the

role of the guardian ad litem is to represent the child's best interests.

In the current statute, the child is generally considered a respondent. This stance appears to create an assumption among guardians ad litem that an adversarial role exists between the cabinet (petitioner) and the child (respondent).

3. Repealing the current statute that grants paternity rights to a putative father solely on the basis of being named in the mother's affidavit.

It was agreed by all advisory committee members that granting rights by mother's affidavit is the single greatest cause of delay in the termination of parental rights process. The committee received repeated testimony that delays were caused by mothers naming a new or different father immediately before the initiation of the termination of parental rights proceedings. Each time a new father was named, proceedings were delayed for several months while a new search was completed. Review of United States Supreme Court rulings indicates that parental rights involve more than simple biological ties to the child [Lehr v. Robertson 1983]; that the granting of parental rights requires some type of action by the father. After much discussion, the advisory committee recommended for repeal.

4. Granting the court authority to terminate parental visiting if it is found to be detrimental to the child.

Visiting between the child and the parent, after the permanency goal has been changed to adoption, is often confusing and painful for the child. Currently, visiting can be terminated upon motion to the circuit court.

5. Reducing the period for abandonment from six months to 90 days.

The committee made this decision because the first five years of life are the years most important for a child's development, and because lengthy foster care placements are inherently difficult for children.

6. Revising the section of the statute dealing with reasonable efforts to require that reasonable efforts be made only until the filing of the termination of parental rights petition.

The statute had required reasonable efforts toward reunification up until the time of the hearing. This change eliminates a confusing message previously sent to children and families when the cabinet decided that the termination of parental rights was in the child's best interests, yet continued to require reunification services. The revision also resulted in the section of the statute dealing with reasonable efforts being rewritten in more clear and concise language.

7. Revising a section of the statute to allow incarceration of the parent to be considered as one factor in determining the best interests of the child if the parent has failed to make adequate provision for the care and nurturing of the child.

The recommendations of the legislative subcommittee were well researched and thoroughly reviewed. The resulting legislative package represents a progressive step toward timely permanence for children, while at the same time recognizing the rights of parents and guardians. The filing of these recommendations was only the beginning of the actual process toward legislative change. The recommended changes will require further advocacy from committee members and others interested in the welfare of Kentucky's children.

Project Outcomes

From the onset of this project, the cabinet has scrutinized TPR cases through its internal monitoring system. Although these cases have always had high priority with the attorneys in the Office of Counsel and the Family Services office supervisors and workers, the monitoring initiated by this project has brought about much shorter time frames. Most significantly, a new time-saving step has been added to the process: the attorney, social worker, and supervisor meet to discuss cases as soon as there is some indication that the goal will be changed from reunification to adoption. Statistics show a 50% reduction in the time from a social worker's notice to the Office of Counsel to the judge rendering a decision. Table 3 shows some of the recent changes.

As the data indicate, the goal of reducing the time needed to complete the TPR process was achieved, and that process has been improved. The list that follows summarizes the major activities and accomplishments of the advisory committee and support staff.

Table 3. Summary of Project Results

Average Interval	FY'89	FY'90	FY'91
From social worker's notice to Office of Counsel to petition filed	112.5 days	20 days	23 days
From filing of petition to trial date	27.3 mos	7.5 mos	4.6mos
From trial date to judge's decision	90 days	56 days	70 days

1. The establishment of a promising DSS automated tracking system for monitoring TPR cases.

    It will track children from the time they enter out-of-home care throughout the period of care, with a specific focus on the TPR and adoption processes. Although the new system is much more thorough than the previous foster care monitoring system, by combining several systems and documents, it actually relieves staff members of paperwork.

    In addition to producing statistics regarding children in care, the new system is also equipped to produce a number of management documents that will alert the staff when any established time frame is not met. For instance, after the child's goal is changed to adoption, the worker has 30 days to complete paperwork for the Office of Counsel. If a specific task is not achieved in this period, the system will produce management documents to alert the appropriate supervisory staff to the problem.

2. The production of a video training tape.

    The video provides a rare opportunity to learn from three teenagers what it is like to be a child involved in an involuntary TPR case. Their perceptions, their needs, and their frustrations with the system are poignantly expressed.

3. Regionalized training to improve handling of TPR cases.

    Three multidisciplinary seminars involved 300 social work-
    ers, foster parents, advocates, and attorneys; a second educa-
    tional program brought in 37 circuit and appellate court
    judges. The training offered a philosophical basis for the
    policy and procedural changes, as well as opportunities to
    discuss and learn through practical application, which con-
    solidates retention of information.

4. Revision of DSS policy and forms concerning TPR pro-
    cedures.

    The preparation of case information for the Office of Coun-
    sel was found to be difficult and cumbersome, involving com-
    pleting an initial request form, writing a chronology of the
    entire case record, locating and attaching multiple legal doc-
    uments, and completing several repetitive forms. On the rec-
    ommendations of a subcommittee, the format of information
    exchanged between the Office of Counsel and the field staff
    was revised. A new request form establishes a simplified pro-
    cess that more closely reflects the evidential needs of the
    case. The new system also replaces the case chronology with
    a single document that charts services rendered. Other pro-
    cedural changes, such as tightening time frames in which
    specific tasks are to be completed and eliminating unneces-
    sary levels of approval, minimized delay in the processing of
    these cases.

    The TPR committee advised DSS that it was the depart-
    ment's ethical obligation to inform all parents of the pos-
    sibility of a termination action when their child enters
    out-of-home care. The following statement will be included
    in all out-of-home care treatment plans: "Your child has been
    removed from your home because the court has determined
    that the risk was too great for your child to be returned to
    you at this time. This treatment plan is designed to assist in
    reuniting you with your child; however, failure to cooperate
    with this treatment plan could result in a termination of your
    parental rights and a placement of your child for adoption."

5. Improving the efficiency and timeliness of the absent-parent
    search process.

    The policy and procedures manual has been revised to
    encourage completion of the search. A new handbook pro-
    vides step-by-step instructions, sample letters, and a national

listing of resources. In addition, the actual manner in which an absent-parent search is conducted has been revised by a staff role change, as described earlier.

6. Shortening the appellate court review process.

    A special priority panel has been appointed to review TPR appeals. Oral arguments may now be waived unless they are specifically requested.

7. Revising the circuit judge's bench book on TPR to include current case law and expanded explanations of the TPR process and statutory requirements.

8. Improving communication between the Office of Counsel and the DSS staff, as detailed earlier.

9. Recommending statutory changes. A bill has been prefiled to revise the section on termination of parental rights.

    The recommendations include:
    • Revise the abandonment statute by lessening the time requirement from six months to 90 days;
    • Revise the putative father statute to eliminate associated delays;
    • Clarify the statutory grounds for termination;
    • Place statutory time frames on the court for TPR hearings;
    • End the requirement that the court appoint a guardian ad litem in all voluntary TPR cases;
    • Make parental visiting after the filing of the petition dependent on the court's discretion.

10. Developing a simplified and updated chart of the TPR process (included as figure 2.)

    This chart is distributed to the staff in the procedures manual and in ongoing training.

11. Initiating two new projects that will be evaluated over time.

    Two pilot districts each hired a permanency planning specialist for three years, beginning in FY '92, to provide consultation to staff members regarding permanency planning, case management, evaluation, and monitoring of the TPR process. The hiring of specialists has been recommended for other counties. Jefferson County, where one-third of the state's TPR cases are filed for hearings, hired a paralegal staff member whose duties include conducting absent-parent searches, assisting in preparation of agency forms, and filing petitions.

Figure 2. Kentucky's Involuntary TPR Process after the Project

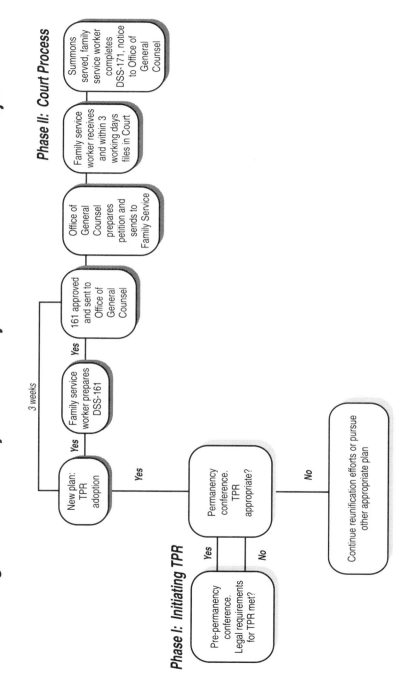

Phase III: Trial

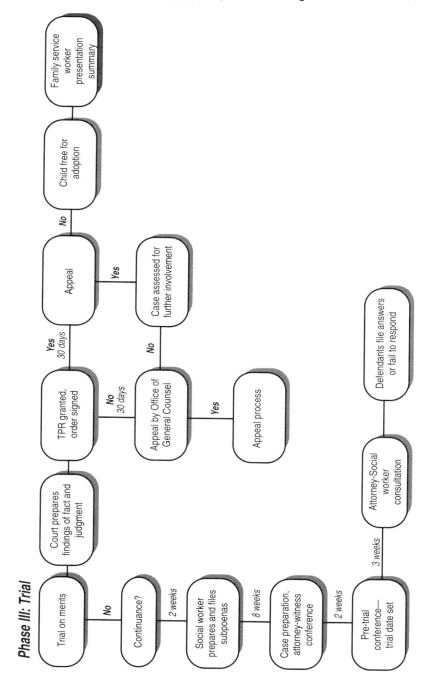

CHAPTER 5

Interagency Collaboration: System Improvements for Planning Permanence

Paul Johnson, Pamela Day, and Katharine Cahn

The professional community that serves children and families in the Northwest's public child welfare system includes social workers, advocates, attorneys, judges, court personnel, and other professionals. Each discipline plays an important role in assuring permanency for children either by reuniting and stabilizing families or by establishing permanent alternatives. Each community has developed ways to collaborate, more or less successfully, in sharing information, planning, and making decisions about the children and families served by the agencies and practitioners in each system. Although most of these people have collaborated in the past, they often have great difficulty reaching case resolution when faced with the complex and emotionally laden decisions around terminating parental rights (TPR) or returning children to their biological parents—decisions that call for intense cooperation and clear intentions on the part of all participants.

This chapter describes a community seminar process that improves permanency planning for children by improving local interagency collaboration, with emphasis on the interaction between the local court and legal professionals and the local public child welfare agency. Recommendations emerging from this experience are offered to other professionals who seek to enhance their interdisciplinary problem-solving efforts for the sake of children in out-of-home care.

Introduction to the Project

The Northwest Resource Center for Children, Youth, and Families (NWRC)* developed an interagency collaboration—Children Can't Wait: A Court-Agency Project—to assist local communities in achieving permanence for children in the child welfare system. In nine communities in the Pacific Northwest, three in each of three states, professionals from courts, agencies, and advocacy groups participated in a seminar to find out what they could do to expedite case resolution and permanence for children.

Removing the Impediments

NWRC designed its seminar on the assumptions that all professionals involved in the child welfare system value the need for speedy permanence decisions and that many of the impediments to changing local child welfare systems to meet this need resulted from (1) confusion about the roles of the various professionals involved in the process; (2) omitting or limiting the involvement of key players in identifying and addressing systemic problems; and (3) lack of awareness among key players of the progress already made in solving local system problems, which common data collection and information sharing would reveal.

Clarifying Roles and Responsibilities

In previous work by the NWRC, judges, court personnel, guardians ad litem, attorneys, and public agency social workers had identified professional differences as an obstacle to reaching permanency planning goals. The professional differences between attorneys and court professionals, on the one hand, and social workers and advocates, on the other, cause conflicts and delays in permanency planning. The unique professional values and perspectives of each discipline often result in conflicting problem assessments, conflicting expectations, and conflicting methods of intervention. Ronnau and Poertner [1989] compared the case perceptions of judges, social workers, and attorneys in child abuse

---

*The Northwest Resource Center for Children, Youth, and Families at the University of Washington School of Social Work provides training and consultation to public child welfare professionals and administrators in Oregon, Washington, and Idaho. The Children Can't Wait project grew out of an earlier training effort in the three states called Partners for Permanence.

assessments and placement decisions. Their research showed that social workers often agreed with both attorneys and judges about the severity of the abuse and the level of intervention needed, and that attorneys and judges often disagreed with each other. Other authors [Lau 1983; Fein et al. 1984; Irving 1981; Katz 1988; Ordway 1985; Duquette and Ramsey 1986] also describe differences among the disciplines that interact to provide services to children and families in the court-agency process.

Involving Key Personnel

All the key players should be involved in identifying and addressing systemic problems. This need is often overlooked. Circumventing the input of legitimate participants in any process will almost always lead to a delay when those who have been omitted enter the arena. Active inclusion will bring together essential views and contributions from many corners of this complex system and will encourage commitment of all to the common goal. Goldstein et al. [1986] discuss the interconnectedness of the many agencies and disciplines that work towards permanence for children and the importance of a variety of professionals to creating and facilitating permanency plans. Sources on team building confirm the need for inclusiveness in child protection and child welfare planning [Schmitt 1978; Skaff 1988].

Sharing Progress

Common data collection can make key players aware of the progress already made in solving common problems. Once a group has set a clear goal to attain, a measure of success in reaching that goal will be a motivator for the members of the group. It may be that key members are unaware of the severity of the foster care backlog or the extent of court docketing delays. Much has been written about the powerful effect of information that is identified, gathered, and shared by participants in a multidisciplinary project [Gugerty 1982; Brunner and Guzman 1989; Nix 1977; Rapoport 1985; Weiss 1972].

Seminar Goals

The core of the project was a seminar held in nine counties in Washington, Oregon, and Idaho. The seminar used an interagency problem-solving process

- To clarify the roles and responsibilities of each discipline;
- To identify both current good child welfare practice and the current obstacles to permanence for children in each county;
- To strengthen interagency collaboration by creating strategic plans to address local impediments in each of the counties;
- To identify data within counties regarding their progress toward timely permanency planning; and
- To describe the project and the process and make that information available for replication in other communities.

Project Components

The Children Can't Wait project had four interdependent components: Consulting Teams, Seminar Process, Strategic Action Plans, and Data Collection and Reporting.

Consulting Teams

In each state, some professionals and advocates had already taken on leadership roles in promoting permanency planning. A number of these leaders were asked to serve on their state's Permanency Consulting Teams.

Each of the state consulting teams brought together key decision-makers from the judiciary, law, social work, and CASA programs. Team members were chosen for their knowledge of the issues, their commitment to improving practice, their leadership capability, and their ability to represent a professional and organizational point of view. Project coordinators looked for participants with varying degrees of knowledge and commitment. Each coordinator tried to include at least one judge who already understood the importance of permanency planning and could influence his or her peers.

The team members met to advise the NWRC on how and where to conduct the in-state seminars. They were instrumental in recruiting participants for the seminars. Local team members identified representatives from the judiciary, parent and agency counsels, the child welfare agency, and CASA programs. State team members met with local teams representing each of the local disciplines and helped to identify and enroll participants from their respective professions. As previous efforts have demonstrated, judges are more likely to attend training if they are invited by other judges, attorneys by other attorneys, and so on. Lead judges and lead attorneys from each state and local team made personal contact with some of those invited to urge their attendance. In all cases, the seminars were scheduled on dates that were convenient for key judges. Also included were court staff members, and, in some cases, an even broader representation of professionals and advocates from the community.

Seminar Process**

The seminar was designed to clarify the roles and responsibilities of each discipline, and to identify current good child welfare practices, vital issues, and system impediments. Interdisciplinary groups were formed to create strategic action plans for removing particular obstacles.

The objectives of the seminar were (1) to build strong working relationships among colleagues from key disciplines serving children and families; (2) to identify obstacles to good practice and share techniques for fostering interagency problem-solving, and (3) to establish a local agenda for achieving permanence for children. Each seminar had six steps.

1. An introduction of the participants and facilitators, a brief history of the project, a statement of purpose, and an overview of the training.

    State or community leaders explained why they had come and summarized state and local trends on children in out-of-home care. This exchange of information was meant to dispel the myth that "We're doing all right," and clarify where the system wasn't working.

2. "Where are we with permanency planning?"—a step that continued the focus on participants' attitudes and knowledge.

    A video presentation, based on the *60 Minutes* story, "Karen's Kids," illustrated the systemic nature of permanency planning and how important it is that all parts of the

---

**This process is also discussed in "Building Court-Agency Partnerships to Reunify Families," by Pamela Day, Katharine Cahn, and Paul Johnson, in *Together Again: Family Reunification in Foster Care*, edited by Barbara Pine, Robin Warsh, and Anthony Maluccio, Washington, DC: CWLA, 1993.

system work. The video was the springboard for a discussion on "Could this happen here?"

3. A section on the common values and the distinctive roles of the various disciplines represented in the room.

Participants met in small groups, by discipline, and agreed on a list of professional goals related to permanency planning. Each group was asked to define its roles in the process. Later, the large group discussed common values and points of difference, highlighting how role differences can create tension and misunderstanding among key players. A variety of interdisciplinary hindrances were brought up, discussed, and recorded in the course of this exercise.

4. Interagency small group meetings.

In each group, participants reviewed a written synopsis of a permanency planning case and reported their recommendations back to the large group.

This exercise used the process of staffing a case to develop consensus on best practice with children and families and to highlight the role that each professional must take in achieving best practice. The exercise was also intended to help participants feel comfortable working as an interagency team.

The cases used for this exercise were based on actual permanency planning cases provided by the participating state agencies. In their small groups, participants decided what should happen with each case and what each person should do to move the case toward resolution. Seminar leaders emphasized that by sharing different perspectives while seeking agreement, participants could come up with the best possible plan for a child and his or her family and each profession in the system could contribute to carrying out the plan.

Much discussion took place among the participants, as both professional perspectives and local biases came into play. The dynamics of the groups reflected the role and professional differences described earlier. The status differences between legal professionals and social workers were played out in one groups' reluctance to overrule a strong judge who was a group member. The win-lose mentality of an attorney in another group prevailed temporarily over the judgment of social service professionals, who had strong feelings about moving a case toward TPR. In other cases, court professionals went along with agency members because it was the path of least resistance or because they trusted the social worker's expertise.

As the small groups reported back, the facilitators helped group members describe the process they used to reach agreement. This was another opportunity for airing differences about goals, values, and professional norms. The facilitators invited discussion from the full group and summarized points of agreement and difference. This discussion brought out specific practice issues for the county, which were also recorded.

5. How each party in the process can take part in improving it.

    Facilitators combined the identified best practices and the local impediments into themes and displayed them on poster paper around the room. Participants walked around adding suggestions for how each professional could deal with each impediment or practice in the direction of improving permanency planning practice. This exercise provided another safe way for participants to express their opinions about the contributions required from each profession.

6. The local commitment to improving practice.

    Participants were grouped together to design strategies on issues that interested them. This exercise is detailed in the next section, Strategic Action Plans.

Strategic Action Plans

Each planning group developed at least one action plan to take back to its community. The action plans specified the responsibilities of each participant, established time frames, and listed anticipated outcomes. Action plans were shared with the full group before the seminar was adjourned.

The seminar facilitators acknowledged the availability of many strategic planning models, some of them already in use by the participants. Facilitators offered an outline of a model that could produce concrete steps toward a clearly defined outcome within the relatively short period of time available in a seminar setting. Each interdisciplinary group had formed around a common concern that was slowing the achievement of permanence for children in their community. Groups were asked to:

- Express their common concern in a brief statement.
- Briefly state the outcome they were seeking.

- Brainstorm strategies to reach that outcome.

- Select and outline at least one strategy.

- Decide what the first step would be; that is, who would do what soon after the ending of the seminar. The first step would produce an immediate accomplishment to guide the group to the next step and those beyond.

- Identify milestones to mark progress, and give thought to who outside the group would be sought for sanction or support.

- Give their action plan a catchy name, to promote immediate recognition and group cohesion.

Following the seminar, frequent monitoring, consultation, and encouragement by the NWRC project staff motivated and reminded participants to continue carrying out their action plans. Direct involvement by members of the state planning teams added further motivation.

Data Collection and Reporting

Seminar participants collected data on the length of time between key decision points in the process from initial placement to termination of parental rights (TPR) for all nine sites. For each child granted a TPR order during the first year and a half of the project, the intervals between four case process milestones were noted: (1) placing the child in out-of-home care, (2) identifying adoption as the permanency planning goal in the case plan, (3) filing the TPR petition, and (4) granting the TPR order. This data was distributed to the participants and publicized in a newsletter to generate discussion and informed action planning.

It was unlikely that the impact of project activities would show up in the numbers collected during this initial period, but keeping statistics from the start of the project established a baseline against which future progress could be measured. Agencies were encouraged to maintain the pattern of interagency data collection and dissemination established during the project.

The sharing of data can be a powerful call to interagency action. If the action plans are successful, the sharing of data will be a useful acknowledgment of progress made towards timely permanence for all children.

Project Results

Goal 1. Clarifying Roles and Responsibilities

Gathering a significant representation from all disciplines in the nine counties was key to the achievement of this goal. The nine seminars brought together 404 professionals: 20 judges or court commissioners; 26 attorneys who represented the agency; 35 attorneys who represented parents; 30 court personnel; 45 guardians ad litem and other advocates; 70 child welfare administrators or supervisors; 73 child welfare agency social workers; 55 community treatment-resource professionals, 12 volunteer citizen review board members; 16 foster parents; and 22 other community professionals from local schools, Indian tribes, and police agencies.

The unique roles, attitudes, and values of each discipline and the unique opportunities the seminar provided to reveal and clarify these elements were woven into the fabric of the seminar, making it an enlightening experience for many of the participants.

Goal 2. Identifying Good Practice and Obstacles to Permanence

Participants described many good interdisciplinary practices they were currently using to speed the system along, but also many obstacles and local interdisciplinary problems that were slowing down the system. Of the latter, the following were the most common causes of delay:

- A lack of clear timelines and specific consequences in court-ordered case plans. Court-ordered case plans were extended when parents were making minimal progress; agencies and treatment providers felt no real incentive to provide immediate effective services for parents.

- A failure to identify potential TPR cases in the early stages, which allowed these cases to linger needlessly with other child welfare cases.

- Neglecting to identify absent fathers and putative fathers early in a case and include them in the planning. Early planning could result in earlier TPRs and also reveal potential kinship care resources.

* Backlogs in court calendaring and court docketing. Continuances, demands on court personnel, and courtroom priorities all contribute to backlogs.

* Postponement of dependency or TPR processes because of criminal prosecution of parents. Often a decision on the facts or disposition in a child welfare case is not sought until a criminal child abuse case or other action has been resolved.

* Lack of efforts to resolve case issues before court actions begin. Precious court time is taken up with legal arguments and testimony about matters that are uncontested or that could have been resolved ahead of time.

* A lack of collaboration in assessment and decision-making. Leaving out key information or key persons often results in having to begin all over again. Foster parents and other caregivers are those most often excluded.

* Not including parents in the planning. Inclusion means involving parents in the assessment and case planning as well as in setting timelines and consequences.

* Lack of agreement on a community-based ''reasonable efforts'' standard. Besides efforts to avoid placement, this standard also includes the setting of commonly accepted parameters for making changes in a child's permanency planning goal. Conflicting views on what constitutes reasonable efforts result in differing expectations and planning strategies.

* Local differences in the roles of attorneys, social workers, court personnel, guardians ad litem, and foster parents. Local professionals bring to their roles a variety of child welfare experiences and assigned duties, as well as their own attitudes and values.

* Overlooking the cultural issues in placement and family intervention, resulting in having to move a child again.

* Gaps in resources, resistance to combining resources, and limited options for funding resources.

* Lack of appropriate skill and knowledge on the part of advocates, foster parents, social workers, attorneys, judges, and others in the permanency planning process.

Goal 3. Strengthening Interagency Collaboration

The participants at each seminar examined their lists of local impediments to speedy permanency outcomes and designed strategic plans on selected issues. The seminar was an opportunity for people who had not worked collaboratively in the past to do so, and for those who had a history of collaboration to clearly define and confidently approach their next tasks.

In the nine seminars, the participants produced a total of 45 action plans. Each plan was unique to one community, designed to be carried out by local representatives from a variety of disciplines. Each targeted a specific outcome aimed at speeding the decision-making process in a county through collaborative effort.

Strategies to Improve Collaboration

Twelve action plans sought to modify interagency agreements or create new agreements that would accelerate the permanency planning process. Seven of these plans produced changes in the system or made headway toward that goal. Twelve plans created interdisciplinary assessment and decision-making mechanisms to reach permanency planning goals. Four plans resulted in progress toward these changes. Ten of the interdisciplinary planning groups are continuing to pursue this effort.

Strategies to Modify the Legal and Administrative Framework

Three action plans sought to streamline the process of reunification decision-making within an agency. All three plans have brought about substantial gains in reaching changes internal to an agency based on the work of interdisciplinary groups.

Strategies to Improve the Practice of Social Workers, Attorneys, and Other Professionals

Four action plans were intended to continue the seminar effort of cross-training regarding the particular values, goals, methods, and attitudes of members of the many disciplines involved in a court-agency process. Numerous trainings and other events designed to provide cross-agency exposure have been developed, and all four of those groups continued to meet to develop additional events with additional professions. Four action plans sought to enhance cultural sensitivity. These planning groups were having difficulty demonstrating progress, but all were continuing to meet to try alternative strategies. Five action plans aimed to provide the opportunity for community professionals to increase their skills or knowledge about particular aspects of working with children and families toward a permanency planning goal. Training designed by an interdisciplinary group has yielded much success for these five groups.

Strategies on Legislation and Resource Funding

Five action plans created interdisciplinary efforts to seek help from government and other funding sources. Two of these groups focused their attention on a particular practice area and made substantial gains in obtaining additional local and statewide resources. Others tried to enroll a broader constituency on a broader set of resource issues delaying permanency planning goals.

Outcomes were accomplished or major progress was made in 26 of the action plans. Of the remaining 18 plans, five were set aside, and participants continued to meet on the other 13. Of the 45 planning groups, 32 continued to meet after the project ended to further their progress or identify new goals to pursue. The appendix highlights a number of the action plans.

Goal 4. Collecting County Data

Many of the participants found the information that was collected both food for discussion and clear motivation for initiating change. Continued information-gathering would enable participants to monitor how their system changes improved the lives of children. It was helpful to illustrate recommendations with a description of how new information can be gathered and used.

Since the only cases examined were those in which a TPR order had in fact been granted, many cases that reached other permanence outcomes were not reported. Some trends were observed, however, in the reported TPR cases.

During the first full year of the project, participants reported 246 cases in which a TPR order was granted. During the first six months of the second year of the project, the participants already had 212 TPR completions to report. (Reporting was not requested during the final six months of the project, but a few of the counties reported another 81 TPR cases.) The reported case data reflect only case time frames for cases in which termination of parental rights and adoption became the permanency plan. In many cases, the permanency plan was returning the child home, guardianship, or permanent foster care. The data do not include the final step of a TPR case—the adoption.

Throughout the life of the project, the reported TPR cases reflected an average decline in the number of months from the initial placement to the decision to seek adoption. Also, during this time period, many of the counties reported an increase in the total time between placement and TPR. The participants interpreted this increase as a result of (1) focusing on more cases and (2) focusing on cases that had been stalled in the caseloads. Several counties developed action plans that cleared up long-term cases. The complexity of long-term cases was reflected in longer average processing times to reach TPR orders.

Since the data collection was limited in scope, a number of questions cannot be answered. For example, it is impossible to tell if case process time frames are affected by factors such as number of caseworkers, family ethnicity, family composition, age of the child, number of previous placements, presenting problem, available court time, or number of attorneys available. Certainly, these factors and others do affect how quickly the system moves children into permanent homes. Changes in service delivery are also not reflected in the data. For instance, the numbers cannot show the growing interest and participation across disciplines in expediting and streamlining permanency procedures, or reflect the system enhancements instituted by the action planning teams the project created.

Despite the limitations of the data, it was possible to discern that the participants were affected by the data collection process. The involvement of the participants in identifying how to collect and share the data contributed to greater attention to the results they sought in their strategic planning. The data served as one of the stimuli to move the participants' discussion of local obstacles to discussion of concrete outcomes. Although the long-range impact of project activities did not show up in the numbers collected during the project period, keeping the statistics from the start of the project established a baseline against which future progress can be measured.

Goal 5. Disseminating Results and Recommendations

Recommendations may be grouped in four areas: building state teams, conducting the seminar, developing action plans, and collecting case data.

Building State Teams

- Build state or local consulting teams comprising respected child welfare professionals within each of the key disciplines: judges, attorneys, advocates, public child welfare professionals, and care and treatment professionals.

    Team members should have the ability, time, and willingness to provide consultation to members of their profession at the local level. State or local consulting team members should have the ability to inspire members of their discipline at the county level to become engaged in the seminar and the planning process.

- Include a wide variety of professions, agencies, and levels of authority.

    Be sure to include parents' attorneys and advocates. The size of the audience is less important than its composition. Positive results emerged from groups ranging from eight to 90 members.

- Choose community areas in which the agencies and systems share common target populations.

    This is usually true of counties, but some regions encompassing several similar counties with overlapping jurisdictions can be appropriate choices.

Conducting the Seminar

- Promote the seminar as a catalytic event that will produce real change in how systems work for the benefit of children and families in a county.

    Emphasize the systemic nature of reunification and TPR and the importance of teamwork. To help participants move beyond blaming and toward problem-solving, the seminar should highlight the importance of working together to make the system work, with built-in opportunities for solving problems successfully so that participants can leave feeling supported by one another and hopeful about what can be done.

- Infuse role clarification wherever possible throughout the process.

    The seminar should include content and exercises focused on goals and values, professional roles, and norms for professional behavior.

- Provide a safe arena for discussion of the issues. A neutral facilitator can encourage objective discussion and get the process going.

  Pay attention to the historical nature of interagency relationships and recognize progress already made. Participants come to the seminars with old wounds and prejudices. They may wonder if they have been singled out because they are viewed as a problem court or problem county. To inoculate against this, a nondeficit, blame-free training environment should be established, stressing the importance of leaving old baggage and organizational history behind and focusing upon common goals. Humor also normalizes the situation, helping people see that differences can be recognized, valued, and even respected.

- Offer a variety of ways for participants to present issues and discuss options, including large groups, small groups, and anonymous written input.

  Trainers and facilitators should model mutual respect and problem-solving. Presenters and facilitators should include state team members representing the courts, the legal community, and the agency. Seminar participants can be given an active role through group discussion, small group exercises, and finally, by being called on to develop a plan for their own county.

Developing Action Plans

- Supply a strategic planning tool that assures continued efforts after the seminar. The plans must have clearly stated tasks and outcomes.

- Maintain regular, systematic follow-up contacts with participants to support and assure progress, to stimulate countywide support, and to assist with adjustments to new and changing issues.

Collecting Case Data

- Seek common accessible data. Choose areas in which the agencies and systems have a common target population, usually a county.

- Identify the most relevant numerical data or other progress indicators and disseminate them to participants. The intent of the facilitators is not to define the indicators but to encourage ongoing sharing of them.

- Base the selection and collection of progress indicators on currently available information that may indicate change as a result of multidisciplinary system change.
- Given the slow development of information systems in the child welfare field, it's realistic to start with what's available and use that data to advocate for better information management in the future.

Conclusion

The interdisciplinary challenge to move children out of temporary foster care and into permanent homes with biological parents, relatives, guardians, or adoptive parents has brought out the best in child welfare professionals. The Children Can't Wait project has highlighted the successes and difficulties that Pacific Northwest communities are experiencing in their efforts to meet that challenge. Federal and state mandates and often-conflicting professional postures make clear the need for improvements in relationships. The project has given communities both opportunity and assistance in furthering interagency relationships. Opening up avenues for interagency work will increase successful permanency outcomes for children in care.

References

Brunner, I., and Guzman, A. "Participatory Evaluation: A Tool to Assess Projects and Empower People." In International Innovations in Evaluation Methodology: New Directions for Program Evaluation, edited by R. F. Conner and M. Hendricks. San Francisco: Jossey-Bass, Inc., 1989.

Day, Pamela; Cahn, Katharine; and Johnson, Paul. "Building Court-Agency Partnerships to Reunify Families." In Together Again: Family Reunification in Foster Care, edited by Anthony Maluccio, Robin Warsh, and Barbara Pine. Washington, DC: CWLA, 1993.

Duquette, J. D., and Ramsey, J. D. "Using Lay Volunteers to Represent Children in Child Protection Court Proceedings." Child Abuse and Neglect 10, 3 (1986): 293–308.

Fein, Edith; Miller, Katharine; Olmstead, Kathleen; and Howe, George. "The Roles of the Social Worker in Permanency Planning." CHILD WELFARE LXIII, 4 (July/August 1984): 351–359.

Goldstein, Joseph; Freud, Anna; Solnit, Albert J.; and Goldstein, Sonja. In the Best Interest of the Child. New York: The Free Press, 1986.

Gugerty, John J., and Getzel, Elizabeth E. "Evaluation of Interagency Collaboration." Exceptional Education Quarterly 3, 3 (1982): 25–32.

Irving, Howard H. Family Law: An Interdisciplinary Perspective. Toronto, ON: The Carswell Company Limited, 1981.

Katz, Linda. Courtwise: Making Optimal Use of the Legal Process to Insure Early Permanency for Children. Seattle, WA: Northwest Resource Center for Children, Youth, and Families, 1988.

Lau, Judith Alphson. "Lawyers vs. Social Workers: Is Cerebral Hemisphericity the Culprit?" CHILD WELFARE LXII, 1 (Jan./Feb. 1983): 21–29.

Nix, H. L. The Community and Its Involvement in the Study Planning Action Process. (HEW Publication # 78–8355) Atlanta, GA: U.S. Department of Health, Education, and Welfare, Public Health Service, Center for Disease Control, 1977.

Ordway, Dustin P. "Standards for Judicial Determination in Child Maltreatment Cases—A Legal Dilemma." In Foster Care: Current Issues, Policies and Practices, edited by Martha J. Cox and Roger D. Cox. Norwood, NJ: Ablex Publishing Corporation, 1985.

Rapoport, R. N., ed. Children, Youth and Families: The Action-Research Relationship. New York: Cambridge University Press, 1985.

Ronnau, John, and Poertner, John. "Building Consensus among Child Protection Professionals." Families in Society: The Journal of Contemporary Social Work 70, 7 (September 1989): 428–435.

Schmitt, Barton D., ed. The Child Protection Team Handbook: A Multidisciplinary Approach to Managing Child Abuse and Neglect. New York and London: Garland STPM Press, 1978.

Skaff, Laura F. "Child Maltreatment Coordinating Committees for Effective Service Delivery." CHILD WELFARE LXV, 3 (May/June 1988): 217–230.

Weiss, C. H. Evaluating Action Programs: Readings in Social Action and Education. Boston: Allyn and Bacon, Inc., 1972.

Appendix

"Children Can't Wait" Action Plans

Strategies to Improve Interagency Collaboration

Twelve action plans sought to create or modify interagency protocols or procedural agreements that would eliminate unnecessary steps and/or would add steps to accelerate the permanency planning process. The plans included these seven:

1. Pretrial Planning Project
    Participants were concerned about the parties in a case not finding out what had been happening on the case until the review hearing. The strategy agreed upon was to hold a planning conference four weeks after a dependency petition is filed. It would be an opportunity for all parties to decide on the specifics of the plan of action. Only contested issues would then be heard in court. Representatives from all disciplines in the juvenile court process have been meeting regularly since the seminar to design the pretrial planning conference procedure.

2. RAP: Rapid Action Petition
    This group is attempting to reduce the time between establishing TPR as the goal and filing the petition from one month to a two-day average. Agreement was reached between the child welfare agency and the attorney general's office that the line social workers would bring their completed reports (defending the need for termination of parental rights) to their first preparation meeting with the assigned attorney. The attorney would then use this report to prepare the petition and file it with the court within two days of the meeting.

3. KIP: Kick in the Pants
    Group members were concerned about significant delays in the court processing of appeals of termination of parental rights (TPR) orders. They developed a way to shorten court processing time by using court reporters rather than tape recorders and subsequent transcription.

4. HERB: Help Eliminate Ridiculous Bottlenecks
    Group members were concerned about significant delays in the court processing of appeals of TPR orders. They de-

veloped strategies to change the law to limit cases to one appeal from magistrate to supreme court.

5. RAP: Relationships with Agency Personnel

This action plan dealt with the problem that dependency cases were being substantially delayed because the Oregon Children Services Division staff had either no legal representation or inconsistent representation in the court review hearings. The agency manager met with the District Attorney and drafted an agreement that provided for representation at all hearings as requested by the agency. This group also devised strategies to include caseworkers who specialized in court activities or the juvenile court staff in processing dependency court cases, a strategy to approach judges to establish pretrial conferences, and a strategy to research other counties where attorneys are being appointed for parents, so that the county could appoint attorneys for parents at initial hearings.

6. HERO: Hold Essential Reviews Only

This group sought less duplication of citizen review board and court reviews and a reduction in the number of all reviews. Strategies included a system to get more information up front so fewer reviews were necessary, ways to prevent loss of information, ways to remove or cancel conditional reviews, and ways to obtain dedicated docket time.

7. FRAM: Faster Resolution Access Module

This planning group sought equal access to the court in a reasonable time period for all parties. Court procedures were modified so that all hearings were scheduled within the parameters set by the Idaho code and rules.

Another group of 12 action plans sought interdisciplinary assessments and interdisciplinary decision-making mechanisms to reach reunification or alternative permanency planning goals. Among them:

1. Roto Rooter: Effective Communication between Therapists, Social Workers, and Guardians ad Litem for Treatment and Referral

This planning group wanted to increase the county professionals' awareness of available treatment and support resources for families. This included shared awareness of the intensity, capabilities, and breadth of mental health resources, and common standards for assessment and appropriate treatment. Progress was made on a format and time frame for reports and assessments from community professionals, and on establishing contract standards, professional standards, and useful requirements for the Division of Children and Family Services and the court.

2. Kid Quest

Participants were concerned with service options for children with multiple problems or disorders. They were to establish a multidisciplinary committee that would identify agencies to share responsibilities and resources, develop a model of diagnosis and treatment requiring a continuum of assessment and care, and create long-term commitment and support from a variety of agencies.

3. MAP: Multidiscipline Approach Project

This group began putting a mechanism in place to assist other planning efforts in the county for children and families requiring multidisciplinary help. This mechanism will include a grant process, a board of administrators, a tracking function, and a capacity to identify clients from a high-risk pool.

4. Fins and Sins: It's a Wrap

These participants found that the each county agency had insulated itself from other agencies, thereby creating obstacles for service delivery to families. Community systems and subsystems were serving systemic needs rather than family needs. They began work on ways to build a common philosophy within the community about serving families in a joint community effort.

5. Rawhide: Head 'Em Up, Move 'Em Out

One office had built a waiting list of children and families in need of TPR planning. Their supervisors and managers and the presiding juvenile court judge agreed to target cases on the waiting list that were likely to be uncontested and to result in successful adoptions. The judge agreed to set aside periodically a half-hour special docket just for the prima facie cases. This avoided a three-or-four-day trial scheduled months in advance. So far, 34 children have been identified, and TPR has taken place in nine cases; three children are in adoptive placements. The agency has found this strategy successful enough to warrant hiring for two positions to screen, select, and process these cases.

Strategies to Modify the Legal and Administrative Framework

Three action plans sought to streamline the steps of permanency planning decision-making within an agency.

1. Refocusing
    The Children's Services branch in this county was redesigning the initial steps of its service delivery system for child welfare cases. Concerned with permanency planning in the early stages, this group strategy incorporated permanency planning and preadoption procedures in the redesign.

2. Name That Tune: Intake Planning for Permanency
    To prevent last-minute revelations of critical information, such as ICWA status or status of a father, this group developed a checklist with a suggested timeline for any case where a child will be in care more than 30 days.

3. RAPP: Rapid Advancement of Permanency Plans
    Group members developed a system of forms and checklists to identify procedural steps that should be addressed at the initial stages of juvenile court dependency actions.

Strategies to Improve the Practice of Social Workers, Attorneys, and Other Professionals

Four action plans were created to continue the seminar effort of cross-training regarding the values, goals, methods, and attitudes of members of the many disciplines involved in the court-agency process.

1. and 2.   Can Do, aka Reasonable Efforts, and Clarity
    Two counties are working on plans to more clearly define the reasonable efforts standard for their respective communities, to reduce the time of processing a case through court and reduce the number of cases with undetermined permanency planning goals. Both county committees have extensively surveyed definitions and case law regarding reasonable efforts around the country. Both are also drawing on opinions from the many disciplines in their own communities about the developing guidelines. The Northwest Resource Center conducted a literature search and provided information to the two sites.

3. Respect

In an effort to gain a clearer definition and understanding of the roles and responsibilities of each party in a dependency or TPR action, participants have conducted a cross-training conference for juvenile court staff, Children's Services Department (CSD) caseworkers, attorneys, CASAs, and others. Before the conference, the CSD office hosted a walk-around session in which two juvenile court judges and all of the juvenile court referees toured the local CSD office and learned about its workings.

4. UCAD: Uncovering Child Abuse Duties

This group sought to eliminate duplication and overlap and fill gaps between county juvenile court staff functions and state juvenile probation department staff functions. Participants planned to develop a flowchart of roles in the current system and catalog the system's history from 1959 on, to redefine wardship and staff roles, to identify areas of duplication, and to make recommendations.

Cultural Sensitivity Strategies

The four action plans that sought to enhance cultural sensitivity in working with children and families and to ensure that agencies are attentive to multicultural issues included:

1. RAP: The Recruitment Action Plan

Concerned that there were not enough minority workers in all areas of child welfare, including family foster parents, guardians ad litem, attorneys, and social workers, this group developed strategies to increase the representation of varied ethnic groups.

2. CIA: County Indian Affairs

Concerned about a lack of awareness of Native American child welfare issues in the county, this group planned a task force to develop workshops with guardians ad litem, Division of Children and Family Services staff, court staff, and other community professionals; to consolidate and enhance current projects; and to recruit and train Native American guardians ad litem and foster parents.

3. The Summit

Concerned about a lack of foster care resources for Native Americans, and about updating the working agreement between the tribes and the state agency, this group set up a series of meetings to fill that gap. Meetings included discussions about how to use Court Appointed Special Advocates (CASAs) within the tribal courts and the community.

Permanency Strategies

Five action plans aimed to provide an opportunity for community professionals to increase their skills or knowledge about specific aspects of working with children and families toward a permanency planning goal. These included:

1. PERC: Professional Education Resource Committee
    Participants planned to provide education for the judiciary and attorneys on child development, children's needs, and permanency planning. This training would be provided by local child development and child welfare experts. Judges and attorneys would provide education for community professionals, social workers, guardians ad litem, and foster parents. Social workers would be trained in a variety of court procedures and expectations. Several specific trainings have been held as a result of this committee's work.

2. SAPP: Substance Abuse Permanency Planning
    This planning group took steps to increase county child welfare professionals' awareness of the seriousness of alcohol and other drug (AOD) problems in dependency and permanency planning, so that professionals would routinely include identification of any alcohol and drug problems as early in the intake assessment process as possible. The first strategies accomplished were designating an alcohol and drug specialist in the Division of Children and Family Services office and assuring that in-depth AOD training is available for members of the permanency planning team.

3. Foster Parent Training
    This multidisciplinary group satisfactorily achieved its goal of assuring mandatory, ongoing training for foster parents. The group identified training needs and inspired participation in training.

4. Training by Judges
    This group decided that the best way to train judges about TPR issues was to provide a seminar that included a panel of judges discussing the issues. A TPR issues seminar was

organized and conducted in southern Oregon for child welfare professionals and others.

Strategies to Address Legislative and Resource Funding Issues

Five action plans created interdisciplinary efforts to impact government and other funding sources, including:

1. The McBC: The New Don McNeil Breakfast Club

   This group of participants wanted identifiable and accessible services for teens. They planned to begin by identifying all the resources and services available to teens in one county, and hoped to use a computerized database, collecting the needs assessments that have been done, identifying service areas not covered, and establishing service priorities.

2. CASH: Children's Advocacy for Services and Homes

   The participants were concerned about the lack of adequate staffing levels and resources in child and family services. This lack significantly delayed the timely conclusion of permanency planning for children. They created a multidisciplinary task force that collected supportive data from participating disciplines to use with the state legislature.

3. RUN: Resources Urgently Needed

   This group was concerned about the lack of money for adequate staffing, training, and services, and especially about gaining additional child welfare social workers for the local office. The participants formed an interdisciplinary group consisting of a guardian ad litem, a member of the Child Protection Team, a foster parent, and a representative from the Department of Health and Welfare to establish a fact sheet of needs and priorities and to seek grants and ways to advocate for increased funding.

CHAPTER 6

Reaching Timely Permanency Decisions: A Recapitulation

Katharine Cahn and Paul Johnson

The preceding chapters make it clear that workable alternatives to foster care drift can be found. Children may grow up to be healthy, contributing adults in a variety of settings, but a sense of safety and secure belonging is invariably essential. In Michigan, Kentucky, New York, Oregon, Washington, and Idaho, collaborative projects were able to promote security for children by changing laws and administrative codes, improving practice, building stronger interagency collaboration, and increasing resources dedicated to helping children and their families. This chapter summarizes the steps that other states can take to improve outcomes for children.

Improving the Legal and Administrative Framework Governing Decision-Making

The projects reviewed in this volume present a strong case for the value of well-constructed policy. Changes in laws, statutes, and administrative protocols made a difference in every state.

Build Shorter Timelines into State Laws

Changes in the law are particularly well illustrated by the experience of Michigan, where the law now requires a permanent plan for every child in care by the twelfth month. In Kentucky, the waiting period for filing the petition on abandoned infants was shortened and stricter timelines were placed on the court for termination of parental rights (TPR) hearings. Although some people feared that the timelines would not allow for adequate reunification efforts, the opposite was true. The aggressive case-work required to develop an early permanency decision has re-sulted in timely return to the family network for large numbers of children. At the same time, other children have been freed for adoptive placement or clearly defined long-term family foster care placement in a shorter period than formerly in both states. When narrow time frames are enforced, they promote good prac-tice for most children in care.

Promote Other Legal Changes

Changes in the laws to allow open adoption, to allow but not require parental visiting after termination papers have been filed, and to ease the divisive impact of the adversarial climate sur-rounding involuntary TPRs were all successful in specific project states.

Herring, in chapter 2 of this volume, and Ratterman, in chapter 3, recommend changes in state statutes to allow legal represen-tation for the agency—as if the agency social worker were the attorney's client—from the early stages of each case. This would furnish attorney support for the social worker, early consultation on case design, and early opportunities for the social worker to discuss the particulars of the case with the attorney. In many states, providing an attorney for the agency social worker would require statutory changes. In other states, attorneys could be made available if funds were allocated to increase the agency's assigned legal staff.

Reducing the time required by statute to declare an infant abandoned produced better outcomes for infants in Kentucky, where an infant may now be declared abandoned if the parent has made no effort to contact the child in 90 days—a significant reduction from the previous period of six months.

Change Court Rules

Even without changes in laws or statutes, improvements in court rules can move the TPR process along quickly and humanely. Each state found, for example, that certain docketing and scheduling problems caused delays. Criminal cases take precedence over dependency cases on crowded court calendars. A dependency case that runs over the scheduled time limit must sometimes wait months for rescheduling. These delays may be tolerable in corporate cases, but they cannot be tolerated when the months of delay are months of valuable time in a child's life. Court schedules should be revised to reflect the critical nature of timely decision-making for children.

Improvements in court calendaring were achieved in several ways. In one Washington-state court system, a day was set aside to hear uncontested TPR petitions, such as those for abandoned infants, so that attorneys and caseworkers, who handled many of the cases, could use their time efficiently. Kentucky recommended adding a priority assignment to TPR cases, and made other recommendations for changes in court procedures that halved the time previously required to review cases.

Current legal process is adversarial. Child welfare decision-making is seldom characterized by clear-cut, win-lose issues. In fact, the best outcomes may be preserved by applying a collaborative, win-win decision-making process at some points, as long as all parties' rights are protected. In one Oregon county, for example, all the parties convene before trial so that the time scheduled with the judge can be used to hear only contested facts, not facts on which both sides agree. The Idaho court system experimented with the use of mediation for some dependency cases, with limited success.

Clarify the Reasonable Efforts Standard in TPR Cases

Although changes in statutes and court rules are needed, nothing will have greater impact on the legal environment for permanency planning than clarification of the reasonable efforts requirement. Public Law 96–272 calls for "reasonable efforts" to reunite the family before placing a child in federally reimbursable foster care. In many jurisdictions, reasonable efforts are also required before TPR. Each project uncovered wide variations in interpretation of the phrase *reasonable efforts*, and differences of opinion regarding the extent to which the reasonable efforts standard applies to TPR cases. The federal intent is not clear, and judicial opinions vary widely.

Where the standard is applied, clarification is needed on several questions. Are there cases—such as those involving infant abandonment, chronic and dangerous mental illness, and long-term incarceration—where TPR is so clearly indicated that no amount of effort is reasonable? Have reasonable efforts been made when lack of funds to provide a resource or the community's lack of a particular resource were the impediments to parental participation? Is it reasonable to attempt reunification or offer services, for the sake of building the best possible TPR case, even when these measures are contrary to the best interests of the child? Judges' opinions on these questions vary from jurisdiction to jurisdiction across the country.

Regardless of the decision on what constitutes reasonable efforts in foster care practice, several authors in this volume contend that the reasonable efforts standard should not be written into state statutes for TPR. Both Ratterman and Herring recommend that state statutes describing the grounds for TPR be based solely on the best interests of the child. They believe reunification efforts should be required insofar as such efforts would support the developmental health of the child, but not beyond that point.

When the best interests of the child would be served by a termination of parental rights, the statute should be written to allow that termination regardless of previous efforts or lack of efforts on the part of the state. The standard for TPR should be the parents' capacity to perform adequately during the rest of the child's childhood, not how well the agency or the parents did or did not perform in the past. Statutory revisions eliminating the reasonable efforts requirement from state termination standards would best protect the interests of the child.

Improve Implementation of Existing Laws

Although an improved statutory and court regulation framework is necessary, laws alone will not solve the problem. The good-faith implementation of the laws is also required. In several states, improvements were noted simply by improving adherence to existing laws and timelines, and by creative interdisciplinary efforts to streamline existing procedures so that they really served the best interests of the children involved.

The best example of this was a project in Idaho to bring all cases into compliance with existing state timelines for hearings and case planning. Streamlining and consolidating the many review hearings involved in dependency cases improved outcomes for children and families.

Improving Legal and Social Work Practice

Improve Practice at the Front End

The best way to avoid long stays in foster care is to keep children out of foster care in the first place or to get them safely back home as soon as possible. It is not surprising, therefore, that steps to improve casework with families when they first come to the attention of the agency were key in all of these projects. The hallmarks of proactive work with families are early assessment of the primary problems putting the child at risk; early identification of all potential placement resources (including extended family resources and putative fathers); early identification of tribal affiliation or other cultural resources; clear case planning that addresses the primary problems; inclusion of the parents in planning, along with explicit timelines for progress and consequences for lack of progress; and early connections with parental and agency attorneys. In Kentucky, parents are clearly informed that failure to cooperate with the treatment plan could result in termination of their parental rights and placement of their child for adoption.

Well-documented, coordinated casework and legal efforts at the beginning of a case give parents a chance to be parents again and also build a solid basis for TPR if all efforts fail. Extra casework staff time and assessment and treatment resources at the front end contribute to better outcomes all along the continuum.

To improve casework at the front end, Kentucky developed a handbook and Oregon's Multnomah County developed a checklist for intake workers. In Michigan, an attorney began to work with a caseworker from the beginning of each case, and stressed the need to conduct thorough searches, to make explicit case plans, and to communicate clearly with the parents.

Increase Technical Skill with Special Problems

Permanency decision-making is particularly challenging when parental progress is hard to predict. These are the cases that tend to linger the longest in foster care, even when parents receive few services or make little progress. For this reason, caseworkers, advocates, and treatment professionals must be given extra training in working with parents who are developmentally disabled, mentally ill, sexually abusive, or addicted to alcohol or other drugs. Alternatively, specialized caseworkers or consultants with appropriate expertise should be available to all caseworkers. In certain cases, legal professionals also need specialized training in permanency planning.

Advocate More Aggressively for Decision Making

One of the reasons children linger in foster care is that the decision to petition for termination of parental rights is hard to confront. To postpone this difficult decision by leaving the child in the limbo of temporary family foster care may spare the conscience of caseworker and parent; avoid the extra work and emotional rigor of taking a petition to court; and appear, on the surface, to spare the child from trauma. Unfortunately, it is the child, growing up in the psychological impermanence of foster care, who suffers most in this scenario. All the projects recommended that social workers, advocates, and attorneys push themselves to do the tough work of making a firm decision. This means seriously questioning the use of long-term foster care and avoiding it wherever possible, and aggressively seeking a decision regarding return home or adoption.

After rigorous examination, some cases remain in which return home is not possible, but termination of parental rights is also not in the best interests of the child. When permanent placement other than adoption is best, the child's sense of permanence should be furthered in other ways. The Michigan project recommended the use of legal agreements among foster parents or guardians, the child, and the agency.

Cases in which such a course of action might be recommended include those in which the parent is incarcerated, termination of parental rights is culturally incongruous or unnecessary, or highly skilled, trained foster parents are prepared to provide a permanent home for the child.

Agencies that specialize in long-term foster care or foster-adopt arrangements have developed some practice expertise in making these temporary situations secure for children. Public agencies should call on these private placement resources, or at least use them as training resources to improve practice in this area. Foster-adopt programs, in which foster parents are prepared to adopt a child if and when the child becomes available for adoption, present many legal challenges, but they have worked well to increase children's sense of security during the decision-making process.

Develop Expertise in Court Work

Many child welfare case workers lack expertise in working with the courts. Preparing a case for court and appearing in court can be alarming prospects. It may be that some of the foster care backlog is fueled by caseworkers' fears of entering the legal arena. Training for all workers in the legal aspects of their job is the first approach to solving this problem. Each of the projects in this volume mentioned versions of such training, from the "How to Survive TPR" training offered in the two New York counties to "Courtwise" for Washington State.

Other solutions to deficits in courtroom skills were also successful. For example, New York and Oregon placed permanency planning specialists in each unit or region to offer consultation on cases moving towards TPR. In Michigan, the attorney assigned to work with the social worker from the beginning of the case provided technical consultation and reassurance for caseworkers on a case-by-case basis. Some areas of Oregon and Washington developed a permanency planning unit that takes all cases for which adoption is the permanent plan.

Develop Judicial and Legal Expertise in Child Welfare

The authors of chapter 1 ranked turnover on the bench and among the ranks of legal professionals with dependency caseloads as a major obstacle to permanency for children. The lack of judicial and legal expertise in dependency matters is a problem that was dealt with in some fashion by all the projects, and all found some benefit in offering training for judges on particular aspects of child welfare timelines and legal work. In the Pacific Northwest, project coordinators offered training at a judicial training conference, and included judges in interdisciplinary seminars and action planning. Kentucky revised the bench book for juvenile court judges. In the Pacific Northwest, several projects explored ways to enable judges with an interest in juvenile law to stay on the juvenile bench for extended periods of time. Otherwise, rotations, sometimes as often as every three months, interfere with the development of judicial expertise on TPR cases, which are not a common occurrence in any but the largest urban areas.

Reduce the Time for Processing Appeals

In some states, appeals of TPR decisions delay cases significantly, adding as much as two or three years to a child's wait for a permanent home. This delay was reduced in Kentucky by waiving oral arguments unless they were requested. In Idaho, appeals were made in an order of priority so that fewer levels of appeal were required in TPR cases.

Address Cultural Variations

Casework practice and legal practice are underdeveloped in working with children from racial and ethnic minority cultural backgrounds. Widespread failure to meet the terms of the Indian Child Welfare Act is a problem across the country. In every project state it was found that workers were not familiar with practice under this act and at best found its requirements intimidating.

Both TPR and adoption take on a different valence in cultures where extended families and nurturing communities have traditionally cared for all children. In tribal settings, as well as in other cultural groups, TPR is feared as an extension of the cultural genocide once practiced by United States government-sponsored agencies. At the same time, Native American, African American, Asian American, and Latino children in the child welfare system do not automatically have access to the networks of support characteristic of their traditional communities. Careful and sensitive assessment of caregiving resources is required.

Much work is needed by culturally sensitive practitioners to develop protections for children within their own communities' definitions of belonging. Areas of culturally sensitive practice explored by the projects in this volume and elsewhere in the country include improving identification and use of extended family placements, improving financial support for kinship care placements, finding new means of assessing these placements, employing variations of open adoption, and drawing on godparents or "parent teams" to provide permanent homes. Right now, too many children of color are spending their lives in family foster care because culturally sensitive practice has not been developed.

Improving Interagency Collaboration

All the projects demonstrated that poor interagency relations caused delays for children, while interagency collaboration held great promise for long-term system improvements and improved outcomes for children. Interagency practice recommendations were presented for all stages of the continuum.

Collaborate from the Early Stages of Each Case

Developing avenues for early contact between social worker and legal counsel proved useful in Michigan and showed promise in some Pacific Northwest counties. Making legal counsel available to the caseworker early on, not just at the point of carrying the TPR petition, can help move the case to a clear permanent decision quickly.

The private attorney model is one mechanism that can provide early contact. Another avenue developed in several sites was a weekly case consultation with a representative from the office of the attorney who takes the case. The smallest example of improving communication methods was the addition of a mailbox for the attorney representing the agency in the agency's office.

Cross-Train

Cross-training, which was characteristic of all four projects, has benefits for practitioners in all systems. In Michigan, adding training from other disciplines to the law school training program increased attorneys' understanding of the child development needs behind social workers' decisions. Child welfare training topics most often mentioned by juvenile court lawyers included the causes and consequences of child abuse and neglect, the developmental needs of children, and some background on the range of problems that families present, such as mental illness and drug addiction.

The Pacific Northwest project demonstrated the benefits of common training programs for all disciplines as an aid to improving working relationships, increasing professional familiarity and respect, and clarifying roles. This approach produces good results when the professionals share knowledge gaps in certain areas, such as drug dependency or the interpretation of reasonable efforts, which can be addressed across systems. Common training is also useful when it focuses on intersystem problem-solving. This type of training builds trust between agencies by providing a time-out in which social workers and attorneys alike can express their frustrations and fears around the court/agency process and gain a better understanding of their common commitment to improving outcomes for children.

Kentucky developed a training resource, the video *Children Can't Wait*, that shows interviews with children who have been the victims of delay in reaching TPR. This or a similar video can be a compelling springboard for cross-system training.

Develop Interagency Task Forces

The previous chapters often mention the value of interagency task forces to promote understanding and problem-solving. Interagency advisory boards operated in three of the four project sites, and continued in some form after the end of the formal projects. Examples range from the very formal, such as the Kentucky state Interagency Advisory Committee, to informal local efforts such as monthly breakfast meetings among court, agency, and review board advocates.

Improve the Interagency Flow of Information

Clearly, a flow of information from one professional to another is essential for the successful resolution of a case. Each project found that better outcomes for children resulted from improved agency-attorney communication. The best results were found when the improved communication included the parents, the foster parents, the advocate, the therapist or other treatment provider, and others with essential information.

The current system in most states is laden with obstacles to permanence. One solution was the development of forms and checklists (such as the TPR Checklist developed in the New York project) to use in preparing cases for review by an attorney or for transfer to another unit within the child welfare agency. These worked best when they were presented as suggestions or guidelines, rather than as "just another form" to make social workers feel that their discretion has been constrained. In one Idaho county, the use of a checklist in transferring cases saved, on average, a month of valuable time in the life of a waiting child. Streamlined forms for case transfer were developed in Kentucky and New York as well.

Interagency sharing of information regarding the progress of cases within the system also proved useful in most projects. Mechanisms for sharing information varied according to the state and its information management system. The most advanced version of information-sharing was that of the Kentucky project, which developed one interagency management information system to track cases involving all divisions. Such systems will be welcomed and used by staff members if, as in Kentucky, they result in a reduction of forms and a streamlining of systems, and if they provide caseworkers with information of immediate value to case-work activities.

Advocacy systems can play a key role in collecting and dissem-inating data. Oregon's citizen review boards make a regular yearly report on the status of children in care, based on the cases their volunteers review.

Newsletters and interagency reports can provide regular "snap-shots" of the effectiveness of the agency in achieving timely per-manence for children in care. Both Kentucky and the Pacific Northwest states developed newsletters that discussed perma-nency planning outcomes and ways to remove impediments.

Clarify Roles

With the proliferation of actors on the child welfare stage, it is no wonder there is mystery, confusion, and resentment concern-ing who does what. Several of the projects reported good results from efforts to promote clarity. Cross-training helps in this regard, as long as roles are clearly defined and just require explanation. In many states, however, substantial confusion and difference of opinion remain regarding the best role for advocates, such as guardians ad litem or CASA volunteers, citizen's review panel members, or members of Indian Child Welfare Advisory Com-mittees. Foster parents also press for the chance to share infor-mation about the children in their care.

The best outcomes for children will result from work that clar-ifies the roles of advocates and caregivers in the decision-making process and allows for the constructive exchange of information among all parties. The leadership for this work must come from agency social workers, who often tend to feel second-guessed or attacked by people they perceive as outside the system. Casework-ers can take the initiative in seeking expanded input into case planning, improved access to records, and streamlined hearings. The caseworker should be seen as the coordinator of many sources of information and advice for a child, not as the only expert.

Enhancing Service Resources

Although the approaches described above can be carried out within the parameters of existing resources, new resources must be developed to produce the best outcomes for children.

Increase Staff to Reduce Caseload Size

Within the limitations of current caseloads, improvements in practice are only possible up to a point. Unreasonably high caseloads are common not only for child welfare workers, but also for the legal staff members assigned to carry the cases through court and the public defenders assigned to represent parents. Effective family preservation and permanency planning casework require small caseloads. Only attorneys and social workers with small caseloads (recommendations are 40 cases per attorney and under 26 for a case-carrying child welfare social worker) have time for inter-agency consultation and thorough case preparation. Many states got results by increasing staffing at certain points in the continuum. For example, Washington was able to clear up the backlog in TPR cases awaiting trial by increasing the number of attorneys general. Then the state added adoption workers to avoid a similar backlog at the next stage of the continuum. Planners must avoid moving children from one holding pattern to another. Children will best attain permanence if sufficient staff time is available all along the line.

Add Funds to Provide More Timely Services for Parents

Many delays are the result of agency failure to evaluate parents accurately or to offer adequate services. This is one point at which the development of resources would enhance both reunification and adoption outcomes. For example, developing the funds to conduct drug and alcohol or mental health assessments for larger numbers of parents facilitated early identification of the primary problem in several counties. Lack of such resources can delay a case and result in surprises at a late date.

Conclusion

Children cannot stop growing up while we figure out how to do our jobs. They are continuing to grow and form opinions and develop behaviors consistent with the world we give them. Right now we are giving too many children lives of impermanence, change, and fear of separation; they will be sure to carry on accordingly. These projects demonstrate that solutions can be found for many of the delays our children are experiencing. Laws and statutes must be improved. Practice must be optimized. Professionals from all settings must learn to work well together. And we must dedicate more funds to strengthening families as the first resort for children. The authors of this volume hope that the work we have done will be helpful to our colleagues in furthering our common commitment to timely permanence for children.

About the Authors

Katherine Cahn, M.S.W., is Director of the Northwest Resource Center for Children, Youth and Families, University of Washington School of Social Work, Seattle. She received her B.A. from Reed College and her M.S.W. from the University of Washington. In the course of 12 years as a trainer and facilitator in the area of improving permanency outcomes for children, she has published articles on managing diversity, family-centered practice, and permanency planning, and has developed curricula for Florida and Illinois as well as her own region. Her current project is developing a collaboration between child welfare agencies and the six schools of social work in the Pacific Northwest.

Pamela Day, M.S.W., is the Director of Family Preservation Services at the Child Welfare League of America, Washington, DC. She received her B.A. from the University of Oregon and her M.S.W. from the University of Washington. Before coming to CWLA, Day directed the Northwest Resource Center for Children, Youth and Families, University of Washington School of Social Work, Seattle, and codirected the National Resource Institute for Children with Handicaps, also at the University of Washington. She has provided consultation and training nationally on family-centered and family preservation services, family reunification, and permanency planning, and has developed training curricula on these topics. Her publications include a recent book for service consumers, *When a Family Needs Help*.

Betsy Farley received a B.S. degree from Indiana State University, an M.S. from Indiana University, and an Ed.D. and an M.S.W. (in that order) from the University of Kentucky. She has spent nearly 20 years in social services and related fields, 10 of them at the University of Kentucky in research and development. For the past six years she has worked for the Kentucky Department for Social Services as a grant specialist and program development supervisor in the area of child abuse and neglect.

David Herring, J.D., a 1985 graduate of the University of Michigan Law School, is an assistant professor at the University of Pittsburgh (PA) School of Law. His other relevant publications include "Legal Representation for the State Child Welfare Agency in Civil Child Protection Proceedings: A Comparable Study," *Toledo Law Review* 24 (Summer 1993); "Inclusion of the Reasonable Efforts Requirement in Termination of Parental Rights Statutes: Punishing the Child for the Failures of the State Child Welfare System," *Pittsburgh Law Review* 54, 139 (Fall 1992); and the *Agency Attorney Manual* (1991), published pursuant to this federal grant research project and available from the author.

Paul Johnson, M.S.W., is a Project Coordinator at the Northwest Resource Center for Children, Youth and Families, University of Washington School of Social Work, Seattle. He received his B.S.W. from the University of Montana and his M.P.A. and M.S.W. from Eastern Washington University. A veteran of 12 years as a child protective services worker and supervisor, Johnson has spent the last four years coordinating interagency projects to improve permanency planning. His writing and consulting focus especially on the need to improve coordination and communication between social workers and lawyers.

Debra Ratterman, J.D., a 1984 graduate of Harvard Law School, is a state training director at the American Bar Association Center on Children and the Law, in Washington, DC. She has been working on the issue of freeing children for adoption since 1987. Following up on the successful projects reported in this book, she is now pursuing the same goals in New York's Oneida, Broome, and Monroe Counties. She has published monographs and legal manuals on the federal reasonable efforts requirement, and provides training nationwide on child welfare issues.